The Disfigured Mask

The Disfigured Mask

(On Every Face)

RUFORD ROYAL MURRAY

To order additional copies of this book, contact:
Xlibris
844-714-8691
www.Xlibris.com
Orders@Xlibris.com
832036

CONTENTS

INTRODUCTION

Throughout the ages, the forces of DOMESTIC VIOLENCE have plagued every aspect of our human existence. Mostly, women have been on the receiving end of these inhumane and torturous acts; by their male-counterparts!

The repercussions of such actions have drastically transformed and disfigured the personalities of these individuals, irrespective of their sexual orientation. In an effort to hide or disguise the pains, hurts, frustrations and emptiness that flood their lives, on a daily basis, they create "new identities" call the "Silent Mask!"

The global nonchalant attitude and heightened sense of insensitivity, to this reality, greatly undermine the protection and services so direly needed to curb these abusive behaviors.

It is the author's hope that this book would be the catalyst in the transformation of our society's thoughts and actions; in the restoration of the respect, adoration, and love our women and men so rightly deserve!

"THE SILENT MASK"

The embodiment of life, within the confines of our daily existence, forces us to live within and behind "**The Silent- Mask**!" The social constructs, governing survival, trump our humanness to be kind, empathetic, sensitive, polite and respectful to each other.

How often, have the above intangible, rare and admirable qualities are over-looked and disgraced? Our earthly aspirations and acquisition of material, economic, political, social, racial power or status usually leave us disillusioned; where happiness and peace don't abound.

Abraham H. Maslow's text, Maslow's Hierarchy of Needs: Understand The True Foundation of Human Motivation, projects man's desire to survive! Yes, the five fundamental aspects of this hierarchy are: physiological, safety, social, esteem and self-actualization. They are the propelling forces, incorporated and utilized by us, in our attempt at fulfilling this survival need.

Evidently, in our pursuit of such, we tend to become very "animalistic-in-nature!" Why is that? That is because naturally, we possess the characteristics of the animals within each of us. The quickness of us to be: cruel, vicious, violent and unkind- in thoughts, words and actions; automatically transform us into that "human-animal!"

The manifestation of our power might or heightened social-status quo is re legated to the accumulation of wealth or material possession or both (which is inclusive of family and education.)

In journeying through the mountains and valleys of life, the non-attainment or attainment of these things usually become very frustrating, confusing, depressing and disheartening. The sacrifices and struggles made to realize these desires, sometimes beg the question, "Is it worth it?" Many times, the forces in life: sickness, down-sizing, infidelity, divorce, death or marriage, natural disaster, relocation are translated into failures, tears, arguments, homicides/suicide and the like; due to total disillusionment.

However, the accomplishment of goals or visions does "present" a false sense and public image of happiness! Also, it accentuates a decoy to the incompleteness of and within us- in search of satisfying our wants.

The above concept is highly solidified and embedded within the poem, "The Mask," by the author and poet, Ruford Royal Murray.

<u>The Mask</u>

So many times we speak so bold
Walk so brisk, with a sense of purpose
Laugh so loud like friends of old
To mask the pains and hurts within us.

See how often we dress so neat
With jewels and diamond almost to the feet
The kindness we share seems so real
To hide the truth behind what we feel.

The words we speak seldom say
The depth of emptiness we face each day
For when we are alone, in silence or sleep
Our comfort of joy is the tears we weep.

Unveil the mask and you will see
Some angry souls in deep misery
For even though we smile so bright
In our lives there is no light.

Daily, we ride on waves of emotional instability
As we search for land, a land of peace
Disguising turmoil of harsh reality
By substituting the pains with ease.

Like a ticking timed-bomb, we lay await
For something, someone to aggravate
The anger and hurt that stain like sin
To unleash the human-animal within.

Despite the material wealth we may acquire
Envy and jealousy consume us like fire
That race within our very being
And manifest themselves in violent scenes.

As we transform into weapons of destruction
How desensitize we seem to our human emotion
But, in spite of the color of our skin
How often the MASK hides what's real within.

The spirit of survival ignites within us a competitiveness! One that isn't constructive, positive nor healthy to the populous' development, betterment or empowerment at large! Why is that? It is so, because it feeds on the negative energies and forces of: jealousy, envy, hatred, insecurity and greed!

The inability to satisfy our insatiable wants and zeal to keep up with The Jones', invigorate and fuel this negative, competitive spirit which **masks** its way into our lives.

Too many times, we are surrounded by people (family, friends or acquaintances) who speak words of well-wishes, but can't wait for failure to befall us. Or, even their warm embrace, clothe with colors of sparkle and grace yet, like wolves in sheep clothing so are their actions forever flowing!

The relationship is further amplified and solidified on support of one's achievement or when something is to be gained from such like vampires in search of their prey, seeking to devour the substance of their existence by means of deceit referred to as friendship.

In embracing the paradigm shift, of the struggles being a part of the process, we must subject ourselves to one reality! That reality is, we must harness our resources and power thereof, to effect positive change in bringing "**Truth**" to the **MASK!**

SELF-DENIAL AS REALITY

In society's eyes and views of thoughts, we all look focus, goal-oriented, stable, accomplished, full-of confidence, and competency! However, on a personal level and deep within, we find ourselves lost, confused, frustrated, insignificant, unaccomplished, and inferior to many situations and people.

The compilation of such harsh and painful reality underscores the real hurt and emptiness that are submerged within our beings. Our inability to confront, accept and implement positive strategies to override these forces, forever imprisons us in this world of denial. I, too, have fallen victim to this harsh and destructive reality!

Denial then, restricts our sense of "**Truth**" and undermines the inspiration and empowerment of light from darkness! Our egocentric and asinine qualities, compounded by our superficial mannerism are major factors that contribute to the blossoming and solidifying of this denial; which then translates into "**THE MASK.**"

Many times, our denial becomes the very force that pushes us into fear of being ridiculed, judged, criticized, ostracized or even victimized! The difficulty in following society's norms, usually impacts our creativity and innovation because of the MASK; which we now internalize as our own reality!

Our distaste to reflect or undergo a self-introspection, suffocates the growth and development of our confidence and competency in embracing this denial-that so mercilessly torture and kill our very strength to realize our better judgment and goals.

The line of demarcation, in our conspiracy theory to our "truth," doesn't present us as the contributors to this belief but, victims. Ironically, the very things that afford us identity and strength of character become the fabric to and of our failure. Why? They do, because in our acquisition of material wealth, our self-worth, image and status are immediately elevated and equated to that of accomplishment and fulfillment of life!

However, once these things are taken away from us, either by natural disaster or other-wise, our self-image or identity deteriorates drastically; because our identity or self-worth is equated to our earthly possessions. Also, due to the precious life style and attitude to others, less fortunate, our "camouflage personality" takes over. We are then reduced to "failure, shame, embarrassment, and public humiliation!"

The hurts, pains, anger and frustrations, even our hatred, are substituted with words and actions of "love" to suppress or escape the harsh reality of emptiness and lost. In suppressing these innate, human qualities, via the above forces, it acts like a buffer and decoy to what is real.

On various levels of our social, human interactions: spiritual, physical and psychological- we resort to becoming addicts of and to unprecedented thoughts or actions.

These "**addictive mannerisms**" manifest themselves from two perspectives of the pendulum: inferior/superior complex, low/high esteem, introvert/extrovert, verbal/non-verbal, violent/non-violent, progressive/non-progressive and so on. Yes, the incorporation of **alcohol**, **drugs** and **sex** are also part and parcel of this "Addictive Mannerism."

The determining forces that greatly impact our "addictive mannerism" inevitably hinge on the perception of the magnitude and gravity of the circumstances surrounding the situation/s.

Many times, in cases like deaths, divorces or financial settlements - or even natural disasters leading to the loss of our human and material possessions, we tend to become shameful, hopeless, confuse, embarrass because of us seeing our investments/ labor going up in smoke or disappearing before our very eyes.

These extreme but, real circumstances push many of us to become self-destructive (suicidal, alcoholics, religious/non-religious, and violent among others. The validation to the above realities is because we place our self-worth or identity in things, as opposed to ourselves and God.

The loss of these things, translate into the disappearance of our assumed identity! Once this is removed or taken away, from us by whatever means, our sense of humanness and self-worth become so volatile that we are reduced to a world of emptiness, hopelessness and helplessness; not to mention anger, shame and frustration.

The above concept is highly illuminated in the poem, **SHIPWRECK**, by the poet and author, Ruford Royal Murray.

<u>SHIPWRECK</u>

Like a ship upon trouble waters
So am I, in this life
Tossing and turning from side to side
Confined to a world of strife.

In search of comfort, comfort and peace
Misery and pain never seem to cease
To every step nearer to progress
Rewards me with heartaches and stress.

As the ship shatters along the shore
So does this bottle upon the floor
For my dreams no longer seem to be
Coming to reality.

How heartless can these feelings be
When subjected to profound misery?
The excruciating pain within
Scars my being as an earthly sin.

The sourness of this cup I drink
As I lay in darkness and think

Leaves such bitter taste upon
My mouth, my lips, my tongue.

Like a thorn in my side
I can't hide
These aches and pains I feel each day
For even with my smiles disguised
My actions say otherwise.

What brutal blows I face each day
Despite the prayers as I lay
Beneath these darkened, starry skies
As teardrops fall from my sleepless. sleepless eyes?

The irony to life is that many things in their initial state of and for our enjoyment ultimately bring us pain, anger, frustration or misery. This trajectory befalls us in many ways! Not only that but, it doesn't relegate itself to any one's ethnic, political, religious, economic, social or geographic location or affiliation.

So many incidents present themselves, as testimonies, to this truth: the birth of a child, the purchase of a car, a marriage, selling of a house, vacation or even a divorce.

DISFIGURATION OF THE MASK

Many of us have seen or heard of people who are called **ADDICTS**.

It is the belief that they are "addicts" because of their overwhelming, gravitational pull to and in executing a continuous act beyond their control; which is detrimental to their overall well- being.

THREE FAMILIAR ONES ARE: **SEX ADDICT/ABUSE, DOMESTIC ABUSE AND ALCOHOLISM.**

Our society's stigmatizations of such individuals are that they are bad and self-destructive! However, these manifestations reflect just the tip of the ice-berg or society's problem to these individuals' inability to accept their accountability or responsibility, their perpetuation and justification to these problems, **NOT DISEASES but, DIS-EASES!**

On a deeper level of behavioral analysis on actions and patterns, the "truth" flashes before our very eyes like the sunshine! That is, underneath the **"addiction"** is the hurt or pain that is being stifled or suppressed; due to the denial and desire **to run from** self and truth.

The reality of males being domestically abused by their female-counterparts, do present some level of "not so true!" On a deeper level of analysis, many males are not only embarrassed to disclose this reality but, see themselves being criticized or considered "less-than a man!"

Many male children have been sexually abused by female members of the family but, were afraid to disclose such information. Why? Because they would have been considered lying or even beaten by the parents for alleging such an act. Consequently, the abuse continued and the children's innocence is not only taken away but degraded and dehumanized; which ultimately led to question of self-worth.

The transformation in many of these males' lives has resulted in them becoming anti-women or homosexuals. In the females' case, they have turned into lesbians. On a deeper approach to the denial or desire not to embrace the harsh reality of such, they resort to changing their sexual organs (via expensive operations.) They then live in this "transgender" role and adapt the characteristics and attributes of the opposite sex in this "new" identity.

These abused males also carry the pains, hurts and embarrassments of being assaulted into their adult lives. Due to their inability of not coping nor coming to terms with the repercussions of this abuse, effectively, many males become abusive in their "homosexual or transgender" life-style. Also, that violent mannerism is also manifested by the females that are "lesbians or transgender" too.

The awareness to this harsh reality, of males being abused by their female-counterpart, does present this "running away from" it as truth and to the life-style that is birth and accepted from it.

Irrespective of the gender or abuse, it must be noted that Domestic Violence is a "learnt" act; either witnessed or intentionally executed by the abused or abuser! The negative mannerism of this "act / lifestyle" doesn't present anything to the contrary!

Too many times, parents are the "initiators, role-models and pioneers" of Domestic Violence! The males, wanting to become "men" before their time, look to their fathers as idols: in thoughts, actions and deeds. Also, the females generally follow the behavioral patterns of their parents too.

Consequently, the resolution process of the parents to an argument does translate or trickle into the lives of the children. Also, the children internalize the responses or behavioral patterns (mostly negative) by the parents. Those behavioral patterns usually include: shouting, vulgarity, hitting, name-calling, throwing of items at each other, slamming of doors or storming out of the house, or breaking-up house hold things among others.

The continuation of these acts, as comical as they may seem or sound, usually does climax into more of a physical and emotional abuse. The birth of either abuse, further translate into separation or abandonment of the relationship as it persists; be it heterosexual or otherwise.

With the advent of The Lesbian, Gay, Bisexual and Transgender/LGBT's lifestyle solidify not only the principles of thoughts but, actions openly, many children find themselves intertwined in the abusive behaviors within these relationships. Too often, the children become part of the abusive chain reaction and also victims to the "sexual violence or abuse" themselves.

In Psychology, this concept of "running away from" is referred to as **Escapism**. The idea of escapism embraces the act of one living a life of denial. Also, holding onto the belief that addiction in and of itself results into something bad or negative.

However, that is not the case, to and in every situation! Some forms of addiction are positive! The overwhelming desire to acquire an education and the persistency to follow your dream-in an effort to "escape" poverty, could be classified as an addiction. Also, the continuous resilience in working, twenty-four seven to pay bills and buy a house does encapsulate the concept of addiction.

Having noted the above ideas, despite all the accomplishments, there exists the presence of **THE MASK!** Many ladies, who are unhappy in their marital or non-marital relationships seek refuge in extra-marital affairs or religious sectors of society. This "**sanctuary**" presents a buffer or shield that hides or disguises their reality of loneliness, emptiness or even lack of intimacy.

This displacement of emotional desires is transformed and provided also by the churches in the forms of comfort and love. Also, the religious ambiance or lifestyle, with the gravitational focus on Jesus, becomes the substitute for physical intimacy and satisfaction thereof.

The reality is, some secrets are darker than others-especially as related to infidelity, domestic abuse, homosexuality, lesbianism, homicides, incest, disease, incarceration and so on. As individuals, for such information to be aired publicly, do present a great deal of fear, shame, public embarrassment and humiliation.

Why? Because the stigmatization that comes with them, usually denotes a deeper and greater problem or failure within the home or society at large. Consequently, this consumption with the presence and fear of failure transcends into behavioral patterns that masked it as "not a problem or everything is all right!"

However, underlying the warm embrace, sweet looking smiles, the big houses or cars, jewelry or even the elegant attires; these tend to be the '**decoy**" from the deeper emotional and psychological turmoil or roller-coasters in which we are trapped and living in!

In reference to Sigmund Freud's mental analysis of our emotions, the id, ego and superego are drastically transformed or mutated into various persona; in light of this "**mask-lifestyle**."

The fact that all of us, live behind this "**MASK**," accentuates the reality that mankind at large is a "**World of Masqueraders**." The term masquerade, by the Merriam Webster's definition falls into two categories:

(1) A social gathering of persons wearing masks and often fantastic costumes and

(2) An action or appearance that is more disguise or show false outward act or pretense.

We, then, are all "**masking**" the real truth of ourselves be it behind: our marriages, jobs, education, economics, political, social affiliation or acquisition.

The stage of life has us performing various roles because of our egos' and superegos' images that have been crushed; by the figment of our imaginations! How often do we find our dreams or goals shattered before our very eyes? Or, better yet, on achieving a goal we experience that our sense of happiness doesn't result in its just objective.

Namely, that of a woman becoming pregnant, to keep a man; a child sexually molested by a family member such as an uncle; or even a couple living in an abusive relationship but, doesn't want to divorce because of the children being affected or going to a foster home. Also, they may not want to separate or divorce due to fear of the public's perception, knowledge or public shame.

The above examples are just three of the numerous cases that are publicly known to be part of our society's downfall or limitations contributing to the "**Mask Syndrome!**"

Some of our "**masks**" look more elegant, vibrant and expensive than others! This drastic difference also creates a "**secondary masquerade!**" Why is that? That is because our egos are now transcended to another level called the "**Superiority Complex.**"

Here, the dichotomy of being "**better than**" surfaces- Superior and Inferior Complex. However, either complex is still relegated to that of the mask. Neither one of our "mask" is better than the other. The reality is, our masks are all "**different**" in nature: shape, color, size, strength, texture etc.

Realistically speaking, we possess many different circumstances or situations that transform us into what we are not, behind the masks!

Our ability to welcome and embrace change, openly and willingly, usually come with a price. That is, the rise and fall, or vice-versa, of our socio-economic and geo-political status greatly impacts the nature of our masks.

Too many times, we are even afraid to unveil our own masks! One may ask, "Why is that?" That is because the unveiling brings to light "**the truth**," real situation or emotional plight we are experiencing and does expose our vulnerability.

The truth is not always welcoming or can be accepted for what it is! That is to say, they are skeletons in each of our closets.

We have circumstances or phases in our lives, be it past or present, that may or may not project us as worthy, capable or competent of such. This perception is then translated into us becoming vulnerable to criticisms, ostracization, humiliation or even self-destruction.

Each one of the above factors does undertake a different "mask of operation" once realized. Our tendency to degrade each other puts us at a disadvantage because we have to "truly look at ourselves in the mirror." Many times, we are quick to judge others without taking an inventory of ourselves: handicaps or limitations, prior to defaming or humiliating the other.

SCARS AND THEIR EFFECTS

The **scars** in our lives are the birth place of and for many of the fears, hurts, pains and teardrops being experienced; regularly. Many times, the negative name calling by our parents, teachers, peers or even ourselves are the footprints to the mask before us.

How many of us haven't been called or done things to; that have impacted us negatively? To such an extent, that they are so vivid in our memories, still alive in us and are carried as burdens or baggages throughout our lives?

I concur that neither one of us has, is immune or exempted from such harsh a reality!

Though we try to suppress or block them from our daily lives, don't we find ourselves haunted by their ever presence and harsh reality?

Numerous circumstances **have afforded us to solidify the mask, from different faucets and places of our lives. In our childhood or adulthood, we may have experienced or taken advantage of physically, psychologically, emotionally or spiritually or all combined in one!**

Many of us, may remember being sexually molested by people we trusted (without our consent and at an innocent age,) beaten repeatedly by an adult (for no apparent reason,) humiliated by teachers or peers (to be called dumb, stupid or foolish,) deprived of food (by those in authority,) abandoned by parents (as those who migrated to other distant lands to escape child support or authority,) bullied (by individuals bigger or more affluent than us,) tragic experience (death of a love one,) lied upon (by those in the higher echelons of our society)or forced into a religious lifestyle (for fear of life.)

The above sentiments present themselves as pictures on the walls of our memories! They come alive, however, in many areas of our lives-when we least expect. The internalization, imprint and impact of these scars never go away!

They become the catalysts, which transform many of us into "**The Quiet-Storm**" behind the mask! This transformation manifests itself in us being **dichotomy-oriented**: introverted/extroverted, violent/non-violent, nymphomaniac tendencies/non-nymphomaniac tendencies, lovable/unlovable, sensitive/non-sensitive, vocal/non-vocal, pacific/rebellious, weak/strong (mentally) atheist/religious, or recreation of our sexual orientation and many others.

Not empathizing, understanding or knowing the roots to many of the above elements or forces, with and to each other, inevitably ignites a "**volcanic eruption**" in us that can be very catastrophic!

Many of us become self-destructive, in ways too numerous to mention!

The manifestations of our demise are found in: the use/abuse of sex, drugs (alcohol,) expressions of suicidal thoughts and actions, humiliation, depression, ostracization, abandonment, defiance to authority, gang war-fares, racial discrimination and the like.

Unfortunately, the above phenomena are like ticking timed bombs, awaiting to be exploded once the mask is forced **to be unveiled!**

The occurrence of such act/s can be triggered by a memory, a word, or even an act!

In **Geography**, the **crust** of the earth's surface can be equated to the mask upon our faces. On exploring beneath the crust, we find layers and layers of soil (**strata**) that are synonymous with the years upon which our physical, psychological, emotional and spiritual abuses have been building up.

Ultimately, we come to the **magma,** which comprises of hot, boiling, molten rocks. The magma, in our lives, ushers in the roots of our pains, teardrops, fears, violence, hate and anger among others! Many times, once these forces are drastically disturbed or troubled, automatically we have an emotional roller-coaster; equated to an earth movement called **earthquake**.

For you and I, our earthquake can be violence, spousal abuse, infidelity, substance abuse, physical or sexual abuse, silence, anger, depression, teardrops, murderation, divorce, marriage, abandonment and so on.

Taking the concept further, the earthquake would sometimes lead us to a **volcanic eruption**!

That is, the spewing out or spilling over of the hot, boiling, molten rocks in the form of a thick flow of ashes and lava; through an orifice into the atmosphere. Ultimately, this flow of ashes and lava fall on the earth and destroys basically everything in their path.

In comparison to the volcanic eruption, in our lives, are our manifestations of these self-destructive acts; that don't negatively affect us solely but, trickle into other faucets of our human existence.

As Eleanor Roosevelt said, "No one can make you feel inferior, without your consent." We may, also, agree to disagree that, pain is inevitable but suffering is optional. However, the emotional rupture and continuous torturing many times scrape, cut and shred the very fabric of our human existence to pieces!

When we are bomb-barded by these overwhelming forces of destruction and degradation what is our resolution? Many times, haven't we had to execute the concept of fight or flight, or cry or hide to rescue ourselves from shame, pain, hurt, embarrassment, violence or crime?

Is it to say, "We are weak or strong?" The "trueness" of such a question is within the person behind the mask! Even if we beg to differ, that we are the product of our decisions as opposed to our circumstances; we can, however, concur that "We can't cross the ocean unless we have the courage to lose sight of the shores," as Christopher Columbus said.

The mask also, brings to the forefront that, "Even in laughter their heart is sorrowful; and the end of that mirth is heaviness," Proverbs 14:13.

Many times, we label and stigmatize our women who have been raped or sexually molested as the contributors to such a cause; as opposed to victims. Also, because of our society's disbelief in and to their voices, on this matter, -the women live a life of shame, silence, fear and self-denial throughout the years.

Unfortunately, many of our women who have been exposed to such harsh reality are subjected to destructive criticisms –even from within! These experiences have left them traumatized or paranoid and negatively have affected their marital, sexual or platonic male/female relationships. Also, they suffer from flashbacks, weight loss/gain, depressions, nightmares, severe anxiety, prolong periods of sadness, continuous crying and hopelessness and even suicidal thoughts.

We find that, years upon years, these women would refrain from interacting or intermingling with men, mostly! However, gravitate to other women, of like exposures- for comfort or intimacy or both.

Too often, we (as a society) or even they themselves are of the opinion that they were the contributors to the cause! Why is that? Because the presumptions include: either they flirted too much with the men/women, dressed too provocatively, were at the wrong place at the right time, they wanted it/looked for it or they didn't say "no!"

The above factors solidify the fear, silence or shame in our women; to the point that they begin living a life of internal pain, hurt, shame and anger being MASKED by smiles, discussions or avoidance of discussions on liked topics.

Also, in an effort to **ESCAPE, BLOCK or SUPPRESS** the harsh reality, traumatized-feeling, public or internal shame or excruciating pain many of our women resort to drugs, suicide, violence, depression, low self-esteem or psychological counseling. These are avenues or programs that primarily alleviate these emotional and traumatic experiences but, the **SCARS ARE NEVER ERASED!**

As the Chief Executive Officer and Founder of Women Empowering Women, Mrs. Elizabeth Lambert Polonio said, "This subject of sexual molestation and rape, is a strong-hold that no one wants to deal with, openly and honestly. This strong-hold has destroyed the church and even killed many souls. I truly believe many people have committed suicide because of the pains and the shame of being sexually assaulted and molested!"

The fundamental aspect of our insensitivity to the plight and harsh reality of these sexually abused or assaulted women or men is our **belief** that **we** are "**different than they are because we are stronger and more mentally-stable not to be subjected to such emotional transformation.**"

This difference, as validated by us includes but, not limited to: stupid, dumb, weak, gullible, loser or even naïve as they are. Consequently, that's why they were raped or sexually assaulted.

However, the unfortunate reality of such acts could befall us, at any given time. We must understand, the "**Mask**" doesn't create itself! We become creators and perpetuators of these **MASKS**!

Many times, the internal pain is so profound, that we ourselves are afraid to confront or revisit the person, circumstance, situation or site of such harsh reality. Evidently, the strength or power necessitated for such is far beyond us! Why? That is so because in trying to **embrace** and **accept** that traumatic and harsh reality (again) we become afraid to reopen the wound or scar in reliving the experience/s.

Also, it presents an unwelcoming atmosphere of self-torturing, degradation, dehumanization and lack of inner-strength. The continuous recycling of such an excruciating pain or act doesn't only numb our senses but, drastically diminishes our self-worth and self-esteem!

ARE THEY OBJECTS OR HUMAN-BEINGS?

This begs the question, "Are they (males/females) seen as sex objects: to be played or toyed with, or to be used, abused or misused like tools indiscriminately?"

We can't fathom the immense weight of shame and guilt these forces present in the lives of these women and men. However, we can agree that the gravity and magnitude of this weight is so overwhelming that many lose themselves in depression, continuous teardrops and ultimately death.

Irrespective of their demographic, religious, socio-economic or geo-political differences, one thing we all have in common is- we are a composition of emotions and matter. This universal commonality runs within the very fabric of the religious denominations; that should be the foundation of and to our spiritual principles and developmental processes also.

However, many followers (inclusive of males) find themselves sexually coerced and abused by those in **"Spiritual Power or Authority!"**

Ironically, those spiritual leaders are the very perpetuators of such heinous and evil behaviors; from which they should be preaching and advocating against. However, because we are afraid to publicly disclose (such harsh realities and prestigious individuals in positions) or put our names at risk, or become victimized by them (due to society's disbelief) such acts continue to be carried out and suppressed or denied by the recipients throughout the years.

Many of our **"alter-boys,"** (during their juvenile years) have been sexually molested at the hands of their spiritual leaders. However, because such individuals or institutions are so highly respected in our society, those in authority continuously capitalize on such opportunities!

Throughout the years, the self-worth and self-esteem of many abused individuals (such as these youths) are greatly ruptured and scarred. In an effort to confront and overcome these harsh realities such as: depression, suicidal thoughts or tendencies, humiliation, stigmatization, counseling and financial settlement institutions like rehabilitation or out-reach centers are used in seeking medical attention to alleviate or get rid of the torture, emotional or psychological devastation to the minds, bodies and souls.

These **"resolution strategies"** present a **"temporary-fix"** to the **hard-core** reality or realities of which **THE SCARS BEHIND THE MASKS NEVER GO AWAY!** The existence of these **SCARS** further compound the inner pains, hurts, embarrassment or depression that ultimately contribute to **THE MASK BEFORE US!**

We start living a life of **lie, denial and self-pity** by **"disguising"** these emotions with superficial acts of comfort and joy! However, in truth, we are hurting and crumbling in our own world of misery and strife.

In the advent, rise and acceptance of **The Lesbian Bisexual Gay and Transgender philosophy and lifestyle, globally**, we see the **MASKS** more vividly and often! We may beg to differ that the choices /decisions made by these individuals led them to these circumstances; or, on the contrary, the circumstances led them to these decisions.

Whichever argument or stance taken, we are still left with a life-style that is **"MASKING"** a deeper world of emptiness, frustration, pain, denial and shame. It must be noted, that this behavioral tendency and acceptance of are highly advocated and financially supported by **THE UNITED NATIONS AND ENDORSED BY THE UNITED STATES OF AMERICA!**

We may beg to differ on all fronts of our human-interactions on asking, "Is it right or wrong for The United Nations and America to endorse and support such a lifestyle? You be the judge, jury and executioner of that!

However, we must be cognizant of the fact that this lifestyle is not relegated to adults only but, has become a major or integral part of our juveniles' educational, economic, political, religious and geographic fabric and existence.

Having said that, we must also note that any level of discrimination of and towards this lifestyle can be punishable by law!

This philosophy and lifestyle are so highly embedded within our societies' socio-economic and geo-political institutions and structures that they have become not only accepted but, legalized; as a **MASK to the truth**!

The transition or paradigm shift of this social-construct is highly amplified and illuminated in the poem, "**AMERICA'S CHANGE**," by the author and poet, Ruford Royal Murray.

<u>AMERICA'S CHANGE</u>

The metamorphosis of America's moral values
Has deconstructed the fabric of its existence
By diluting and dehumanizing the fundamental dues
That should be given to life in its reverence.

Its insensitivity and acceptance of such transition
Are in dire need of radical intervention
The absence of sound principles governing a nation
Ultimately climaxes into destruction.

The acceptance of wrong becoming right
And right becoming wrong, morally,
Has birth the concept of "normality" into light
That has undermined its dogmas naturally.

Its influential power, globally,
Is the venom which poisons this world
That epitomizes this nation's functionality
Despite its military and economic twirl.

The forces and instruments of change
Hide themselves behind the arms of the law
By manifesting and justifying a derange
Inconsiderate, negative, and destructive flaw.

How often have the tentacles of injustice
Victimize, immortalize, and dehumanize your society
Within the framework of this,
A thought she calls "**national security**?"

In pursuit of life, justice and liberty
The fundamental principles of this society
Ironically, we are victims of their creation
Having defeated the purpose of this nation.

THE MASK'S MORPHOLOGY

The morphology of this drastic transformation into our main-stream society is of epic proportion and beyond belief! Our **MASKS**, then, become the buffer between what's real or unreal. Too many times, our analysis of someone's reaction/s becomes the bases of our judgment- to what is **TRUTH.**

However, what is **"real"** or **"true"** to the naked eyes usually is a figment of our imagination and manifestation of the hidden, confused and suppressed identity!

We have seen where celebrities, too, are not immune from such harsh and destructive reality! Many of them, live in a world of denial and non-acceptance to the above reality. They resort to drugs or sex, especially **to MASK** their insecurities, failures, hurt and pains and even power!

The incorporation of rehab centers or programs like counselling or twelve-steps don't afford us the **"fix"** or **answer** to resolve the inner-most problems in **unveiling the mask, truthfully and totally!**

The **acceptance** to this harsh reality or problem, in and of itself, empowers us to break free from this chain of bondage and slavery! On concurring with the Japanese writer, Haruki Murakami, "pain is inevitable however, suffering is optional."

This **admission or acceptance** doesn't **erase** our **scars** but, it **unveils the masks** and presents to us the gravity and magnitude of the **roots** and **manifestations to the MASKS!** In unveiling the masks, however, doesn't happen over-night nor is it an easy thing to do!

It requires supernatural strength and divine intervention; which we don't possess!

Consequently, this is where "**we let go and let God**!" This is not to say, we are weak or strong, religious or not but, we are mindful of our human strengths and limitations- of which this is why and where we "**surrender all to Jesus**!"

Yes, in "**surrendering, accepting and unveiling the MASK**" we become **vulnerable**! Why is that? That is because we become open to criticism, discrimination, rejection, persecution or humiliation and a host of many other negative acts; by families or friends or even enemies.

We find that many of us are not prepared and willing to be "**stoned to death**" for and to the repercussions of this vulnerability. Inclusive of this vulnerability, is the courage to publicly disclose the **predators** or **perpetuators** of such harsh reality. This could be male or female from different walks of and echelons of our society.

These are among the forces, then, that transform them (women/men) into a "**different person**" **of character or gender behind THE MASK**!

We, as immigrants to the United States of America, live daily behind the "**MASK of Demographical Assimilation**!" Due to our survival needs, many of us have had to change our traditional way of life: be it our attires, our names, form of communication, sector or habit, hubs, political, social or religious affiliations.

This transmigration, has led to the displacement of many of our fundamental family's standards, values and beliefs. It is imperative to note, that in acclimatizing and assimilating into a "**new culture/world**" many of us had to suppress or disguise our "**true identities**." Not to say, we abandoned them! No, No!

However, our need to and for survival, trumped our principles, cultures, beliefs, norms, families and even our nationalities; to realize our dreams!

Many of us claimed citizenship via documents that weren't ours, got married to individuals (who we wouldn't subject ourselves to) just to legalize our status, took or got jobs using others' identities and information, falsified legal documents to acquire homes or means of transportation, were homeless/jobless (months upon months,) "kicked-out" of family homes by our own flesh and blood, did jobs that were beneath our academic or practical knowledge and experiences among others.

The transformation and recreation of our **MASKS** also manifested itself in: the appearance of our attires, hair-cuts gotten, changes in our verbal/non-verbal communication, cars and homes purchases, crimes or gang interactions, the people we affiliated with or even the geographical locations we started living in.

We, may have been criticized, victimized, ostracized or even marginalized because of us marrying or having children outside of our race or nationalities, socializing with other people unlike us, not cooking or eating our cultural dishes (due to cultural shock/incorporation,) or not interacting with family members (due to differences of understanding) and numerous others.

Our sociological metamorphosis and assimilation weren't readily transparent nor automatic but, intentional! We had to **become a survivor** by virtue of our necessity, social constructs and institutions of the "**new society**!

If our memories serve us right, didn't we experience calling other immigrants to our respective countries derogatory names like: foreigners, aliens, leach on our health programs, threat to our democracy or way of life, burden to our economy, thieves of our jobs, murderers, "Spanish/blacks?"

In doing so, many of us felt and looked at ourselves as being "superior or better than, or more socio-economically and geo-politically stable than our counterparts. To compound these "**figments of our imagination**" we became insensitive, irrational, non-sympathetic, non-empathetic and inhumane towards them; without acknowledging the negative impacts of such actions on their overall well-being.

Many of us, didn't provide them the human-qualities of: love, respect, appreciation, courtesy or decency of social appreciation or support in their "**new society**." So, they too, had to embrace a "**new identity**" or **MASKED** who they were to survive under the tyranny of our inhumane thoughts and actions.

Ironically, as immigrants, we now find ourselves confronted and being exposed to the very inhumane acts and negative name calling; once employed by us! The suddenness of such harsh awakening and reality, brings us to terms of us wishing to be respected, treated as human-beings, provided some level of sensitivity, granted the opportunity to work/live, assimilate into the society/health programs without any form of degradation, dehumanization or discrimination.

In achieving the above objectives, the gradual transformation of ourselves results in the creation of "**new identities**" embedded within the manifestation of the **MASK**.

It must be noted, in an effort to escape or suppress our limitations, hurts, pains and frustrations; due to our negative forces: victimization, ostracization, humiliation, marginalization we undergo a rapid change of "**self-evaluation**."

This heightened level of "**introspection**" forces us to revolutionize our perspectives on others and ourselves in light of our needs and future endeavors; in unison to **THE MASK** being created and worn if we are to live or succeed within the social constructs of our society behind the **MASK**.

Another factor that contributes to the creation, development and solidification of the **MASK IS DOMESTIC VIOLENCE!**

If we were to take an inventory of our lives, where do we see/find ourselves within this poem, **TENSION VIBRATION**, as the **VICTIM or ABUSER/CONTRIBUTOR/ PERPETUATOR?**

TENSION VIBRATION

The facial expressions speak so loudly
The voice from her inner being
As teardrops trickle slowly, quietly
Pain of sorrows flashes like a mystery scene.

So cold as ice is the silence between them
As the tension rises, overflowing from her soul

And cutting through submerge veins within
Like a double edge sword
Destroying everything.
Though he tries to hold her close
Words of anger and sweet distaste
Immobilize his movements with just one dose
As hatred slaps him across the face.
As she transforms into this vicious beast
Ranting, raving and raging so violently
He asks himself, "When will this madness cease?"
As he runs away, hastily.

As she rushes behind him out of control
Like a wild fire, burning and
Scorching his very soul
The fiery fury blazes from her eyes
While grabbing, pushing and
Kicking his very thighs.

The crowd looks on at the chase
Not with laughter nor joy but,
With great distaste
Seeing two people so sweet as can be
Perfecting each other as the enemy.

Where is the LOVE, I once knew
That held me captive to your SWEET EMBRACE?
For here I am running, running from you
My Angel of Love, with a DEVIL'S FACE.

THE IMPACT OF DOMESTIC VIOLENCE

Whichever side of the pendulum we may have found or seen ourselves, present to us a harsh reality; that we are living and exposing ourselves daily to the forces of "**DOMESTIC VIOLENCE!**

The magnitude and gravity of the above word or term encapsulate and manifest the "**human-animal**" within us! In reference to its definition, Wikipedia defines the term, **Domestic Violence** as "a pattern of behavior that involves violence or other abuse by one person against another in a domestic setting, such as in a marriage or cohabitation." It is also named Domestic Abuse, Battering or Family Violence.

For clarification purposes, we must be cognizant of the fact that not only adults (heterosexual or same-sex) are subjected to Domestic Violence! It does involve violence against our children or the elderly, too! Also, it comes to us in so many forms: **Physical, Verbal, Emotional, Economic, Reproductive and Sexual abuse.**

We, inclusive of men, must be mindful of the subtleties of these forces and signs of "**Domestic Abuse.**" Also, in understanding or over-standing them, our socio-economic, geo-political and sexual relationship can be healthier and longer lasting!

Let us, then, look at some of these signs more in depth:

<u>PHYSICAL ABUSE</u>

Physical Abuse can be classified as any laceration, disfiguration or injury to any part of the body that surfaces due to an outside or personal application of force; on one or more occasions.

It has been noted, that many of our women have experienced such act/s at the hands of their families, spouses, friends or even enemies; without realizing that in and of itself, that it's physical abuse!

The following does amplify the point: In a very heated-verbal confrontation, many times it transforms into the licks or blows being thrown by either the male or females upon each other in the forms of : kicks, punches, slaps etc.

Once these acts, do come in contact with their bodies, in and of itself, it is physical abuse. Why is that? That is so because these forces result in the bodies being bruised, cut, scarred or shown signs of abrasions, imprints of fingers, broken bones or even rupturing of anal or vaginal cavity due to forced or unwanted forced entry.

Many of our women, in spite of this abusive behavior, find themselves subjected to it out of fear, intimidation, public humiliation or self-identity complex.

Consequently, a lot of the men, capitalize on these factors and perpetuate these acts; without much assistance or intervention by the authorities or knowledge thereof.

<u>VERBAL ABUSE</u>

This factor embraces a negative statement or remark that is said to or about a person to defame, humiliate, ridicule, or intimidate the person-in an effort for the person to feel less-than or worthless.

The perpetuator or abuser usually becomes the deciding factor or person in deciding or dictating what conversation or types to be entertained. Also, those statements are laced with derogatory remarks that would trickle through jokes, blames, accusations, name-calling, degrading or intimidating remarks.

These remarks are more vibrant and explosive during moments of arguments. Either party, would be calling the other: bitch, dumb, ass, jack-ass, stupid, idiot, fool, bastard, waste-fuck, you won't amount to anything, you good-for-nothing and so on.

Many of our women, are continuously bombarded by these derogatory and dehumanizing remarks; that because of the "power and potency" behind and within these words they (women) become emotionally paralyzed, stigmatized, ostracized or even marginalized within this lifestyle or abuser behavior.

EMOTIONAL ABUSE

In conjunction to the **VERBAL ABUSE, THE EMOTIONAL ABUSE** becomes a by-product of and manifestation of their effects on the ego and superego of the person's psychic!

As Maslow's Hierarchy of needs noted, one of man's needs is that of "self-actualization/self-esteem." However, many of our women (inclusive of men) are continuously degraded verbally and physically that result in internal abrasions, scars, ruptures and ir-repairable life-time devastation!

Again, the focus or objective in dishing out these actions and words include but, not limited to: negatively impact the abuse, to lessen the abused self-confidence or self-esteem, lead to social withdraw or ostracization, create a loss of interest of enthusiasm or even that of depression.

In reiterating, some of the words that are verbalized in the **VERBAL ABUSE** section, find themselves within the creation of the **EMOTIONAL ABUSE**. Here, we see that the women are repeatedly called: dumb, stupid, bitches, waste-fuck, good-for-nothing, embarrassment, foolish etc.

The above derogatory words do ignite in our women an emotional imbalance: due to their overwhelmingly power, counter-productiveness, dehumanizing, self-destructive, embarrassing and creating of insecurity and non-confidence in their strengths, potential and self-worth!

(This element will be further expounded upon, on dissecting and discussing effects of DOMESTIC ABUSE on our children.)

However, research studies have shown that children who have been exposed to DOMESTIC ABUSE/VIOLENCE, carry scars into their adulthood-as a replica of their past experiences.

It must be noted, that because many of them viewed this behavioral patterns as normal, they too execute and manifest these abnormal behavior patterns as the "normal" or "way-of-life" into their relationship.

As parents, we fail to acknowledge that our children are hearing and seeing these actions but, due to their innocence, respect or fear of being chastised, become silent or isolated from us. Also, due to their "masking" of the embarrassment or pain on their mothers' behalf, our women are left stifled or restrained in their developmental process of these children.

Consequently, we see many of our children becoming gang-affiliated, incarcerated, pregnant, drug dealers, prostitutes, homeless, school drop-outs, or abandoning homes all in the name of "disguising these pains" now presented as a way of life called "**THE MASK!**"

Our children's inability to cope, understand or embrace these forces usually lead to many of them to believe that they contributed to such parental actions as opposed to them being victims.

Our women tend to find themselves detested by their children whom their love should have been bestowed upon. Why? That is because many of these children become helpless in the face of these adversaries. Also, many of these women aren't knowledgeable as to how to communicate or relate to these abusive actions to these children's level of comprehension.

In light of that, these children's self-esteems are drastically reduced due to their negative perception of a dysfunctional and abusive home or relationship.

As a people, community or even as an individual, we fail to realize how much of an impact DOMESTIC VIOLENCE/ABUSE affect our children; that they too grow-up "masking" the truth by becoming abusers or perpetuators themselves!

Why is that? Well, many times during the courses of these domestic abuse, the children either see themselves as the cause of the incidences or as to withdraw themselves from the situation or action (however, in seeing or hearing distance.) Also, because they (children) are emotionally connected more to the mothers- their internalization of the pains, hurts and humiliation are greater!

Consequently, the children either incorporate or internalize these behaviors as o'k and perpetuate them in their lives at schools, work or play. Also, they become defiant, bullies, abusers or develop suicidal thoughts and leave their homes earlier than required. Coupled with that, many of the kids present physical confrontation to their fathers/ stepfathers and ultimately end up incarcerated or dead.

We must be cognizant of the fact, that though the children may provide us an attitude consisting of smiles, respect, laughter, courtesy or obedience- these are only filters to their "MASKING" the truth.

Yes, we can concur, that not all of them being exposed to **DOMESTIC VIOLENCE** turn out to be self-destructive! Some translate these experiences or exposures to become advocate against DOMESTIC VIOLENCE, lawyers, teachers, parents or ambassadors against such intentional and abusive behaviors! However, much of them still live within and behind that MASK!

Also, we find that many of these children also translate these scars or social-human abrasions into their own lives as: children, adults, parents and members of society. Either way, our female children sometimes become prostitute, lesbians, suicidal, or prisoners of themselves and the males transform themselves into homosexuals, gangsters, robbers, prisoners, drug-dealers among others to this harsh reality!

The gradual social disintegration of our moral values has negatively impacted and distorted our global infrastructures within every fabric of our human existences!

It is imperative to note, that such disintegration has fostered the perpetuation of the abuses confronted especially by our females. The identification of a fractured bone, determination of areas of unhealthy tissues, traumatic brain injury, tissues' scars, developmental anomalies, identification of multiple sclerosis and other infectious diseases can be shown by the usage of Computed Tomography Scan or Magnetic Resonance Imagery (CT Scan/MRI.)

Neither one of the scientific technology, however, can identify the "pain" or "see" the scars present or created by the very destructive forces of these abuses upon or within the abused!

Irrespective of the time frame or source of the abuse, the presence of the "pain's" or "scar's" existence does create a "quiet storm and weapon of mass destruction" both internally and externally to the individual being abused.

The effects are not readily apparent always! However, the transformation and manifestation of a person's erratic mood swings, sudden physical attacks, verbal accusations, continuous silence or gestures of anger or vulgarity are "clues, cues or even voices" to this harsh and ever present reality!

Too often, the disclosure of these abuses is not forthcoming! Why? Because the victims find themselves as becoming stigmatized as the "contributors" to these causes, the enforcement agencies are not credible and willing to effectively and efficiently intervene in resolving these issues and fearful of being exposed further to repercussions of such acts.

Many of the repercussions include but not limited to: death threats, demotion, ostracization, stalking, abduction of children, burning down of properties among others; that make them vulnerable to the abusers.

Having been a victim of these abuses, within my marriage, has solidified my understanding, empathy and resolve where Domestic Violence and its venomous tentacles are concern. Also, my ability to identify with many of our victims, have strengthen my resolve in writing this book!

The presence of these "pains and scars" of these abuses, especially that of the emotional one can be equated to that of a tooth-ache! Many of us can identify with "having a tooth-ache!" We proclaim the following: "It hurts", "It is painful" or "It is pinching!" During such moments, "it" forces or brings us to tears, screams, frustrations, anger, provides inability to talk, eat or even drink! Doesn't it?

However, with all these bodily reactions or effects, we still can't "see" the pain of the tooth-ach nor can we deny its presence or existence!

Why? That is because it is "invisible!" But its "invisibility" doesn't negate its reality and the negative effects caused by its presence!

The continuous taking of pain killers: Moltrin or Advil, or even antibiotics don't get rid of the pain but only "mask" or alleviate it temporarily. The very pain makes our very existence miserable, unbearable, uncomfortable among many others! Though we may "disguise" the pain's existence or presence in our mouths/lives it still "haunts" our very beings.

We may drink or take drugs excessively, deny ourselves of food, hibernate or isolate ourselves from people, places or things but, the ever presences of this "pain" or "scar" of such abuse doesn't disappear! It persists and exists within us; like our very shadow that we can not run away from (no matter how hard we try or where we go!) So this is what EMOTIONAL ABUSE is to our lives!

REPRODUCTIVE ABUSE

What is REPRODUCTIVE ABUSE? For many of us, inclusive of men, that sounds foreign or even unheard of! However, this is a term used in today's medical community that focuses on a threat or act of stopping a woman or delaying her access to contraceptive for creating a high level of fear in deploying the following tactics:

(1) Hiding or throwing away her contraceptive
(2) Injuring her to the point of a miscarriage or
(3) Rupturing the condom in an effort to get her pregnant.

Many of our women, in spite of using condom during sexual intercourse, are alarmed to find out that they are pregnant! To their amazement, on checking the condoms, they have discovered punctures or holes on them! Also, many of our women have miscarriages due to physical injuries to their bodies by their significant other, or found that their contraceptive weren't available (upon not wanting to get pregnant!)

Evidently, most men find this act of terrorizing, frustrating, demoralizing, dehumanizing and even abusing our women and enjoyment that leaves these women in emotional and psychological distress or depression.

Also, many men have threatened to end or leave the relationship or harm our women if they ever were to call authorities or disclose these acts to the public or, publicly disclose them as perpetuators of these acts.

Consequently, our women live their lives in a "silent-zone" about these acts and pretend outwardly that everything is alright, publicly!

However, on the inside, they are so mentally devastated, emotionally paralyzed and psychologically destroyed that all they do is cry themselves to sleep, resort to alcohol, infidelity, support groups or church, self-depression among others; to escape the pain, hurt, embarrassment or shame.

Many of them (women) even become more self-destructive than others by succumbing to suicidal thoughts and tendencies! Especially, for our women who have lost their children via physical actions by their mates, that have led to miscarriages! Also, they become so isolated, psychologically disfigured and emotionally imbalanced for most of their live. Again, the objective here is to stifle or suppress the pains that are brought upon by these intentional and abusive behaviors.

We must realize, that these abusive and abrasive behaviors are intentionally orchestrated and implemented but, more so rooted, in our men's inability to embrace the women as persons as opposed to objects.

Also, many of these men themselves perpetuate these acts with the knowledge and understanding of what they are doing to our women! However, if they were to envision these women as: their sisters, mothers or even their daughters filled with emotions like themselves; then that wouldn't be.

On reiterating, many men have lost touch with the "humanness" to: love, respect, appreciate and adore our women as living human beings! We may beg to differ, that many of our women don't provide us or themselves anything basically to love, respect, appreciate and adore no more than what is between their legs!

However, that is only skin deep and shallow thinking! We need to look within our women for their rare and intangible qualities of their being: sensitive, warm, appreciative, nurturing and fragile! In understanding their roots, of who they were and now are- that would create a better relationship and rapport with them.

On the contrary, our women have to live daily in denial by disguising their pains, scars and hurts behind teardrops and suicidal thoughts and tendencies in the form of "THE MASK!"

<u>SEXUAL ABUSE</u>

Many of our women (inclusive of men) have been taught, "Don't let anyone touch you, down-there or back there!"

The concept of "down-there or back there" refers to our sexual areas, private parts or genitals. That is inclusive of the vaginal or anal cavities. To our dismay, many sexual intercourses be it vaginal or anal are "forced-entry" on a continuous basis and without the other party/s approval or consent.

This act, doesn't necessary entail the usage of the penis as the entry object but, it hinges on any other device or object that can be used. Such examples include the fingers, toes, vegetables (cucumbers or carrots,) and so on.

Evidently, this behavioral tendency, usually is carried out with the objective of degrading, dehumanizing or incapacitating our women's or men's ability to perform physical, sexual acts by rupturing, bruising or chafing the vaginal or anal cavities.

The news media, research studies, personal interaction and conversations with numerous of our women, have shown to be sexually abused by their spouses, mates or "rapists."

These acts occur where the men: being unemployed, self-depressed, frustrated with their lives, are authoritarians or dictatorial in the homes or are "drunks" use these factors not only to justify but, to sexually exploit their mates-in spite of their refusal or opposition.

Evidently, we find that these men become perpetuators or abusers leading up to their infringement on the children's privacy by transforming into **pedophiles** themselves.

Wikipedia defines the term, **PEDOPHILE**, as a medical form of a psychiatric disorder where an adult or older person experiences or promotes a primary, exclusive sexual attraction to minors or children.

Amazingly, many of our women are too fearful and "in-love"; that they subject themselves and children continuously to this heightened, barbaric and intentional abnormal behavior.

Personally, I concur as much as it may be **PSYCHIATRIC** in nature but, 95% of it is fueled and propelled by an **intentional, behavioral act of power of aggression and suppression**. Also, it must be noted, that these acts are usually employed by people who great trust has been bestowed upon by spouses, family members, acquaintances or even the children themselves.

The fact that these continuous, unwanted, forceful and non-consensual sexual acts occur, inadvertently lead to bruises, chafing or even scarring of their vaginal or anal cavities. Consequently, culminating in the bleeding or discharging of bodily fluids from such impacts.

Unfortunately, many of our females carry these scars as harsh experiences, psychological or emotional and physical burdens or baggage for years with them (even up to adulthood) in silence!

For many, **THEY MASK** these inner-pains, hurts and embarrassment by resorting to: endless days of teardrops, alcohol, prostitution, isolation, violence, or even suicidal tendencies or acts. Also, some of our women and men suppress these traumatic thoughts or experiences in transforming into lesbians, trans-genders, homosexuals, alcoholics, becoming part of some support groups or rehabilitation centers or even advocates against Sexual Abuse of Women/Men and so on!

Also, some of our women have recently had the courage to publicly disclose not only the abusive, behavioral acts but, the abusers/perpetuators by names, socio-economic and geo-political affiliations! In light of that, they, women, have brought them (abusers) into the public's eyes to answer to and under the judicial system for such heinous acts.

Consequently, many perpetuators have either lost their reputations, jobs, destroyed their marriages or relationships, had paid some hefty fines, incarcerated or both for these abusive behaviors.

However, not many of our women are prepared to risk their lives, children, jobs, relationships or even reputations in an effort to "**criminalize**" these perpetuators. As a result, they (our women) continue to live their lives in shame, pains, hurts and embarrassment within and behind the **MASK**!

Also, many children, in becoming adults found it unthinkable to even mention their "**private-parts**" or about someone even touching "**down-there.**" Or, much less calling out that person by name, place, work or position in society!

WHY? Because many of these perpetuators or abusers were and are people of high, social status and respectable individuals in the communities like: principals, teachers, police-men, priests, doctors, soccer-coaches and so on.

These individuals were considered to be very dignified, respectable, role-models, people of integrity and of high esteem in the societies- that such acts were seen as beneath and unheard of by such individuals. Consequently, because of their positions, class and status, many parents have chastised their children as a result of accusing such persons of those heinous, traumatic or unbelievable acts!

Evidently, we can safely see why many of these acts and perpetuators become the "**hidden-hands**" of sexual abuse among others; leaving our females (and males) traumatized and paranoid of such harsh realities and individuals.

Some of our women, have known to find the strength to forgive their abusers or perpetuators; through religious affiliation or support groups.

The above forms can be subtle or coercive and ultimately lead to physical abuse/violence. We may concur that our women, globally, are more the victims of and experience more severe forms of this violence than their male counterparts.

Research has shown us that domestic violence is among the most under reported crimes worldwide for most women. Also, due to the social stigmas regarding male victimization, men face an increased likeliness of being overlooked by healthcare providers.

If a survey were to be done, about battered or women fallen victims of domestic violence, we would be shocked!

Many of our women, being fearful of their male-counterparts live a life of "lie, shame, hurt, scars and pain" **behind the mask**. As we expressed, previously, domestic violence comes and presents itself in many forms. Also, they are many signs that are associated with this harsh and prevalent reality, that are very subtle in shapes and forms.

The composition and complexity of this phenomenon usually cause most of our women to **mask/disguise/desensitize/numb** their inner pains and scars of this behavior or lifestyle. In "masking" this reality, we have seen where the abusers/perpetuators not only **capitalize on the fear** of our women but, **escalate** their practices or behavior to **physical violence** or **ultimately death**.

Also, many of our women, in heterosexual or same-sex relationships are intelligently, physically and economically independently sound: mind, body and soul! In light of that, they still fall victims to such harsh realities!

However, emotionally, we have seen where that has been the weakest link in the destruction, degradation and dehumanization of our women. Many of these women, being possessed of beauty, body and brain embrace relationships from very conflicting angles.

In dissecting this observation, our women, seemingly equate love to the manifestation of the disbursement of tangible gifts and words of appreciation. Sex, however, for many of them is the expression, conformation and endorsement to and of that love.

In relationship to their counterparts, both words are equally interchangeable and possess the similar definition in their eyes! However, the relationship, be it marital/non-marital, heterosexual or same-sex manifests behavioral patterns of domestic violence- where one party begins to be domineering, intimidating and manipulating over the other.

The manifestations of these three forces or elements are seen in relationships where either our women or men are the financial bread-winner, more physically developed, stronger in belief and voice, politically or socially empowered by law and the like. On a larger scale, however, many of our women are more so abused by their male partners.

In an effort to salvage their relationships from social stigma, criticism, embarrassment or even public shame most of our women end up recreating a "**life of disguise**."

What is this life of disguise? This "life of disguise" presents itself as The Mask.! That mask presented, is that of laughter, joy, fabrication of stories to deny and desensitize themselves from the truth as to say, "all is o'k," when asked "how is the relationship, kid, husband or wife doing?"

How often, haven't we seen our women with physical manifestations of abuse, or listen to their cries of emptiness, loneliness, hunger for love, low-esteem, inability to socialize, call friends, visit friends or even spend their own money or said their mates call them derogatory names?

Why is that? That is because many of their male counter-part restricts, coerces, threatens or degrades them emotionally! The above scenarios are all manifestations of symptoms or signs of this deadly, behavioral pattern.

Also, because many of our women don't want to be humiliated, ridiculed, criticized or seen as weaklings or enablers of such harsh and inhumane behaviors, they present a **MASK** and **hide** themselves **behind the truth**!

Surprisingly, many of these women "**justify**" the behavioral pattern and mask by introducing those flaws as mistakes and internalizing them as their personal errors, contributors to the acts or their own reality! Also, they **validate** or **justify** these injustices as: he didn't mean it, we were playing, I fell or that is love!

Even if they were to involve the authority or request the intervention of the law, many of our women try to recall or drop the charges because of guilt or fear of losing their relationships or other futuristic repercussions of violence. Ironically, they would depend and try to protect those very abusers from being incarcerated or sanctioned financially or both! Also, due to this uncertainty, many are continuously subjected to these horrific lifestyle and behaviors.

In conjunction to that, the complacency of living a certain / prestigious lifestyle- these relationships are overwhelmingly undermined by these symptoms.

The development, identity restructuring and internalizing of these injustices as "the norm, it's ok" solidifies the MASK on these faces of our women and men.

It is imperative to note, DOMESTIC VIOLENCE embraces a violent confrontation between or among families or house-hold member involving physical harm, sexual assault, psychological or emotional or all of them!

The social structure of the family includes: spouses, children, former relationship as related to blood. It is so often that our women experience acts of violence or severe behaviors including: threats of emotional intimidation, psychological abuse and isolation by perpetuators or abusers who use coercion as weapon of control over them.

The violence or abuse may not necessarily happen often but, may remain a hidden and constant form of terrorizing them. As previously expressed, DOMESTIC VIOLENCE is not relegated to physical or sexual violence but, also psychological violence among others.

Many of our women (also men) experience and are subjected to this level of violence which is a composition of intense and repetitive degradation, creation of isolation and controlling of their actions or behaviors of the individuals-through intimidation, coercion, or all of the above to their demise.

Unfortunately, we can agree that **DOMESTIC VIOLENCE** not only undermines the family structure but, has been the contributing factor to many untimely deaths. Too often, we ask ourselves, "How come we didn't see those horrific or harsh behavior patterns in him/her sooner?" In response, these negative behavioral acts are very subtle in their presence, manifestations and the gradual incorporation of "coercion techniques becoming fundamentally embedded in the overall relationship.

"POWER OF INTRUSION"

As individuals, we must be mindful that these subtle, negative, behavioral patterns in Psychology or human-social interactions are called "SYMPTOMS" of abuse! Surprisingly, the most frequently employed symptom is the **MISUSE OF POWER AND CONTROL.**

On an average, women find themselves as victims of these circumstances, more often than men. Why is that? This is because, there exist either an economic, psychological or authoritative imbalance within the social fabric of the relationship; where one makes more than the other or "trumps" the authorities of the matter.

In the acquisition and deployment of this power, there comes an overwhelming gravity of control over the other person. The book, Animal Farm, by George Orwell embodies and amplifies this concept of power! In a nutshell, it shows **"POWER CORRUPTS AND ABSOLUTE POWER CORRUPTS ABSOLUTELY!"**

Social observation of our women heightens the reality that most of these women become victims of this feature and resort to isolation, depression, murderation or continuous sense of low self-esteem/ worth or suicidal tendencies.

The above repercussions contribute to them becoming and manifesting a "different lifestyle" to disguise or hide the physical or emotional scars or pains behind the masks. The women, in masking these intentional, unhealthy and negative behavioral patterns are also subjected to a great amount of verbal degradation and humiliation.

It must be noted, that most women don't fully understand, know or acknowledge the "subtle signs" of **DOMESTIC VIOLENCE**, tend to see themselves as "loved" in their relationship or contributors to the cause. That shouldn't be!

To better appreciate, understand and empower our women, let us share some "signs" or manifestations of DOMESTIC VIOLENCE; that must not be taken lightly!

These signs include but, not limited to: **Physical/Sexual, Coercion, Children, Economics, Intimidation, Threat and Religious.**

<u>PHYSICAL/SEXUAL ABUSE</u>

In elaborating on the above concepts of Physical or Sexual Abuse, the premise to either one is an "unwanted and forceful act upon a person, without his or her consent."

This "unwanted and forceful act" includes but not limited to: touching, commenting or gesturing in a manner that embodies an assault or harassment on the recipient/s and resentment thereof.

Most of the time, our women are subjected or subjugated to these attacks in the streets and place of employment: military, police-force, teaching, offices and the like; by their male-counterparts. Not only that but, many are targeted as sex-objects and are forced into sexual activities; with the belief that their bodies will reward them faster economic and up-ward mobility in their aspirations of material wealth or status-quo.

On the contrary, many of them have fallen victims to these "figmented -imaginations" that have been greatly internalized as their reality! Consequently, in the process, many have become: impregnated, dehumanized, degraded, rejected, ostracized or even murdered by the very beliefs and people that held them captive.

Unfortunately, we see that with their dreams not accomplished how painful, embarrassed, humiliated and even heart-wrenching that is! Especially, when many of them had envisioned themselves as managers, directors, principals, or administrators and the like in high paying jobs or businesses!

Evidently, such harsh a reality or even the scars created and left by such tragic experiences are forever haunting that ultimately lead up to endless nights of teardrops, pity-party, shame, suicidal thoughts or even acts of that nature.

In an effort to: escape, disguise or hide the shame, hurts, private or public humiliation or embarrassment many of our women relocate to places, people and things leading up to a complete recreation or transformation of themselves!

The "**why**" has been answered! However, what about the "**HOW**" factor? The "**HOW**" factor embraces numerous and endless thoughts: they change their names, dress differently, ostracize themselves (from familiar people, places and things,) resort to alcoholism, lesbianism, homosexuals, drug, prostitutions or even killers (suicidal or homicidal,) among many others!

<u>COERCION</u>

The term, **coercion,** simply means to force someone to do what he or she wouldn't normally do; by deceit, lies or bribe!

However, if we were to use New Concise Oxford English Dictionary, 11 Edition, **Coercion** is defined as the act of persuading an unwilling person to do something by using force or threat!

Many of our women have given up their virginity, womanhood, or bodies via coercion! This method is used as a weapon by men, in forcing or compelling the females to have sex with them if they want money, material wealth, or profess to love them among other things.

Here, again, because many of these women believe that they need or can't live without a man, his earthly possession, or out-do the other women (in beauty, body and grace,) or manifest their true love via sex they subject themselves not only to sex but, sexual abuse and exchange sex for love and love for sex!

Ultimately, many of these women find themselves pregnant (with unwanted children,) out of wed-lock, infected with some sexually transmitted disease, abandoned, humiliated, homeless, on the streets or even killed in proving how much they love or are in love!

Also, this force becomes so compelling that many of our women become prostitutes, drug dealers, murderers, drug addicts, irresponsible parents, alcoholics or even pedophiles.

Unfortunately, we see that many of them find themselves also becoming sex-slaves, female-traffickers, or murderers in the process of succumbing to this harsh reality in an effort to **MASK** the internal pain, hurt and shame.

In acknowledgement of the above forces, many of these women are trapped by the economic revenues generated and the prestigious life-styles shown (as quickly attainable) but, live in a world of fear of not doing or doing what have been forced upon them!

<u>CHILDREN</u>

We, as a people, community or even as an individual, have failed to realize and accept how much of a **negative impact DOMESTIC VIOLENCE/ABUSE** affect our children! Many of these children, they too grow-up "**MASKING**" their lives and the truth in becoming either abusers or perpetuators.

Why is that? Well, many times during the courses of these "domestic abuse" the children are present, either see themselves as the cause of these acts or even imitate these acts. Also, because they (children) are emotionally connected to their mothers (especially the boys-as scientifically proven) their internalization of the pains, hurts and humiliation are greater!

Coupled with the above, because many of the males would normally run to their mothers' aid or defense during such times, they too become "animalistic-in-nature." As a result, the violence further escalates in their "fighting off "the dads to rescue the mothers from the physical attacks or ill-treatments.

Also, the children either start to incorporate or internalize these behaviors, as ok or theirs, or become defiant, bullies, abuser, physically confrontation to fathers/step-fathers, develop suicidal thoughts and tendencies, leave their homes earlier than expected, incarcerated or dead!

We must be cognizant of the fact, that though these children may provide us an attitude consistent with respect, love, smiles, laughter, courtesy or obedience- these are only filters to their "**MASKING**" the truth!

Yes, we can concur, that not all them (children) being exposed or experienced to **DOMESTIC VIOLENCE** turn out to be self-destructive or an embarrassment to themselves, family or society! Some have translated their experiences in becoming advocates against **DOMESTIC VIOLENCE**, lawyers, teachers and ambassadors against such intentional and abusive behaviors!

However, how many of them are still living within and behind that "MASK!"

We find that many of these children transform these scars or social-human abrasions and abuses into their own lives as: children, adults, parents, and -members of society and leaders in our socio-economic and geo-political structures!

Either way, our female children sometimes become prostitutes, lesbians, killers, introverted, prisoners or even prisoners of themselves!

<u>ECONOMIC ABUSE</u>

The term "Economic Abuse" entails the intentional intimidation and forceful control of one partner over the other's access to economic resources which diminishes or undermines the victim's capacity to support himself or herself and forces the abused to be dependent on the abused or perpetuator!

This level of abuse has been in existence for centuries- as in the case of "**PIMPS!**" In assessing term, "PIMP/S" we come to find out that it denotes a person who controls prostitutes and arranges individuals called clients for their sexual favors and taking most of their earnings in return.

In taking the concept of "pimp" further, it brings to the forefront a business transaction between the provider (PIMP) and client (PROSTITUTE) for a service (SEX.)

Evidently, prostitution is the business or practice of engaging in sexual activity in exchange for payments: either as money, goods, services or some other benefit agreed upon by the transacting parties.

In the absence of a PIMP, if the women just market themselves and receive the payments for services-then it's not an **ECONOMIC ABUSE!** Sometimes, however, our women are mistreated, abused, misused and under-paid for their services. Unfortunately, **ECONOMIC ABUSE** is not relegated to prostitution but, to non-marital, or marital couples in a relationship too!

Our women, mostly are suffocated, stifled and suppressed by men who are very dictatorial, intimidated and domineering in nature to the point of: controlling our women's access to money, maintain earnings or allowing them to acquire or gain financial independence. In compounding the problem and reinforcing the economic abuse, the men interfere or obstruct opportunities for a significant amount of their females' work performance, education or ability to work.

These forces are deployed in a very hostile and insensitive manner- especially where either mate is insecure, jealous, possessive or domineering in the relationship. Many males (in their relationships) have known to: damage their spouses' vehicles, physically disfigure their wives/mates, stolen their bank/credit cards or use coercive means to enforce and perpetuate this heightened and intentional act of abuse!

Also, these men would burn or destroy their mates' valuable documents: for employment, voyages and the like; thereby preventing them from either getting or keeping a job.

In so doing, an automatic domino effect is created: where our women are forced to solicit or sell their bodies for money, they don't have any voice in the financial process or decisions of the homes, the men take away their money or are even forced to MASK their living expenditures in providing checks and balances of any money spent or earned.

Too often, our women are subjected to this act but, they hide behind it with a smile-as if everything is all right! Many of these women can't even buy themselves anything without first consulting or acquiring their mates' approval or endorsement.

This pattern of abusive behavior and intentional act is common within relationships where the self-esteem is low or the fear of losing a standard or luxurious type of lifestyle.

Consequently, to maintain such and **hide** that **fear, many** women not only subject themselves but, entertain the lifestyle to "fake-the-funk" or disguise their hurts, inability or imprisonment to such harsh reality!

Many times, if this abuse persists, we find that the relationships either end in: divorce, isolation, suicidal tendencies, abandonment or infidelity. Either of these defense mechanisms is a "MASK" to the truth of scars, pains, continuous teardrops and humiliation created because of the abuse!

INTIMIDATION

In keeping within the frame-work of **THE MASK BEFORE US,** the term intimidation simply put is an unlawful act of intentionally coercing or frightening an individual to do (or not to do) something against his or her will.

It must be noted, that intimidation runs parallel to bullying or threat; where these negative tactics are used in making or creating **fear** and in return **submission or compliance** by the other person to adhere (or not) to one's demands.

I submit to you, that we have been intimidated in some shape or form and at some point or juncture of our lives! In narrowing it to the **MASK,** however, many of our women have fallen victims and are in very "intimidating relationships;" which are intentional, toxic, unhealthy, destructive and abusive on the perpetuators' or abusers' part.

Intimidation, as previously noted, aligns itself with the idea of threat- which the fundamental premise is to create fear that ultimately leads to submission or compliance!

Many marital relationships manifest these negative forces or energies in the forms of: the perpetuators or abusers drive badly to subdue their women in keeping quiet (in fear of losing their lives,) throwing, smashing or destroying their properties to instill fear and submission (in making evil gestures or comments,) using isolation or limitation for them outside of sexual intercourse, refusal of driving opportunities (because of insecurity,) denial of vacation benefits to harass them, or the taking away of the children if sex or other favors are not rendered.

Most of the time, our women are manipulated and dominated by their mates so much so that: things that they want to see, buy or do are dictated and determined by their male counterparts (if they either do or don't withdraw or gravitate from or towards certain people, places or things,) they are been accused of infidelity or checking up on them as to whomever they were with or talked with!

Also, many of these women are subjected and bullied by mates who use their physical size and strength, verbal aggression, financial dominance, academic or material achievement as ways of degrading, humiliating or embarrassing them.

These negative and derogatory actions or remarks are further "internalized" and solidified in the minds and lives of many of our women; that they are translated and embedded into and as their own reality!

These forces of "internalization and solidification" also show their vicious and ugly faces in situations like: **Divorce and Child Custody!**

Let us examine them briefly, as they relate to "**THE MASK BEFORE US!**"

1. <u>**DIVORCE**</u>

Too often, we see how "intimidation" becomes a deadly, unhealthy, and destructive weapon or tool in the divorce proceedings of a married couple. The assets and liabilities (inclusive of children) become the pawn in the negotiation process; with one party usually becoming domineering, arrogant, non-cooperative, confrontational, insensitive and vindictive towards the other or issues deliberated on.

A couple examples in reinforcing this concept are embedded in these statements:

(A) If I don't get the car or house, you will not be able to see or get the children,
(B) I won't sign the divorce papers if you don't accept my proposition of selling the house.
(C) If you can't buy me out of the business, I will liquidate it.
(D) I will report your illegal and fraudulent activities to the authorities if you don't sign these divorce papers.
(E) You will not get to visit the children if you don't relinquish your parental rights.

The knowledge and fear of not seeing your kids, house taken away if finance not shared equally, or disclosure of illegal or fraudulent activities to the authorities are forces that usually weaken and immediately push our women (mostly) to yield or submit to their husbands' demands.

2. **<u>CHILD CUSTODY</u>**

Many parents, either married or not, often times use their children as pawns as it relates to **CHILD CUSTODY**. The term, CHILD CUSTODY, is basically a judicial judgment or order made by a judge in providing legal, parental and physical care of the children.

Often times, if the women are not economically, mentally, materially or physically stable or capable to provide for the overall well-being of the children- then the male counterparts trump that opportunity.

Emotionally, our women then become very distraught and devastated; when the ruling or order doesn't provide them the victory during the court proceedings. Also, mentally, many of them find themselves developing suicidal tendencies, frustrated, depressed, crying continuously, embarrassed, feel unworthy and incompetent of being mothers.

In conjunction to the above dilemma, numerous women manifest a great deal of fear, of losing their children and children's love thereof; to another woman or the system to be mistreated or raised by either one and the uncertainty of the socio-economic and geo-political repercussions of ever seeing their children again.

To further compound the situation, many of these women are greatly paranoid in wondering what type of negative images their mates may paint of them to their children; or their own children's view of them. Inclusive of that, is the type of legacy they would leave behind.

In an effort to desensitize or hide these overwhelming pains, emptiness, disillusionment, frustration and suicidal thoughts and tendencies, anger, embarrassment and the like-we find many of our women become hopeless, helpless and not to mention depressed.

This sense of depression send many of them into psychiatric institutions, rehabilitation centers, ostracization, alcoholism, isolation, shelters or even develop suicidal tendencies and thoughts all in the name of **MASKING THE FACE BEFORE US**; in suppressing, hiding, detaching and desensitizing themselves from the truth of these intentional and harsh realities!

THREAT

The term "threat" as defined by Webster's Universal College Dictionary is a declaration of an intention to inflict punishment or injury as a warning of probable trouble.

This concept encapsulates **fear** of the unknown, in the recipient/s minds as to the uncertainty, gravity and magnitude of what may transpire! Consequently, that fear pushes and forces many of our women to quickly accept and succumb to any sexual advances or abuses; in an effort not to be killed instead.

The 'fear factor" can include but not limited to: torture, degradation, embarrassment, dissolution of relationship, kidnapping of children, closing of financial accounts, divorcing, burning of homes, reporting of illegal activities to the authorities, death and the like.

How often, haven't we seen or heard of many unknown women (by name or origin) have been killed or disappeared because of their involvement in a crime, activity or relationship; or, their children have been kidnapped, killed or both?

Unfortunately, these are just examples of real life's scenarios that validate the above concept.

In the case of our women, "threat" is often used by men as a sex-tool or manipulating form of acquiring things with or without bodily harm or injury. It has been noted that knowledge is power! The one that has that "power", at his or her disposal, usually employs it in an arrogant, domineering, discriminating and manipulating manner; against the abused.

The relationship between men and this concept is that they marginalize, ostracize and capitalize upon our women's demises and limitations (with these illegal acts) to dehumanize, degrade and subject our women to public and private shame and humiliation!

Some of our women have been able to out-rightly ignore such injustices and defamation of character and personality. However, not many of them are bold, strong and adamant in defending themselves and their values, reputations or risk their emotional attachments. Consequently, they quickly succumb to this harsh and intentional violent reality via sexual acts.

The surrendering or succumbing to sex, quickly, becomes the tool to "silence" the embarrassment, degradation or public humiliation; that would have been created-had such knowledge or information be disclosed.

Such knowledge or information could have included rape, an abortion (multiple,) embezzlement, prostitution, sexually transmitted diseases, incest and the like. These scenarios may seem or sound alienable to many of us! However, in deliberating and acquiring information from many women (whose names I pledge not to disclose due to confidentiality) have been exposed and are product of one or more of these negative forces.

Many of our women have been "threatened" by elderly family members, friends, acquaintances or strangers! In an effort for the divulgement of information not to reach their mates', parents' or other persons' of respect, they were seduced into having sex at an early age and under duress!

Also, they had lost their virginity, at such an early age that they are: afraid of sexual activity, have transformed into lesbians, trans-genders and the like. On asking why? The resounding answers carry the common thread of "**to mask**" the pains, hurts, shame and embarrassment of such an outrageous, heart-wrenching, unforgettable, terrifying, haunting and abusive experience.

Evidently, many of them have noted that they had to: flee from their home lands (to escape the continuous replaying or haunting visions,) cry endlessly, try to kill themselves in an effort to "run" from this harsh reality, decide on murdering the abusers or perpetuators (but couldn't locate them,) denounce having children, fear of sleeping (due to them been traumatized,) become alcoholics (to desensitize or numb the harsh realities,) become trans-genders to inflict the same pain or injury to another (because of the change,) some refrain from sexual activities (due to the harsh memory of the pains and bodily injuries) and others have affiliated themselves to the religious lifestyle to escape, desensitize or mask the harsh realities experienced.

Again, however, these outlets are only known and seen as the scars, hurts and pains that have been and are **MASKING** the deeper and underlying roots or issues to **THE MASK BEFORE US!**

Too many of us have: laughed at, scorned, ridiculed, degraded or even disgraced our women; who have fallen victims to these abuses (inclusive of verbal, physical, emotional and sexual assaults or threats!)

I submit to you, that until and unless we are "personally confronted or exposed to or become victims to these harsh realities, only so would be able to fathom the gravity and magnitude of the negative repercussions caused by them.

<u>RELIGIOUS</u>

The religious component, of and in one's life, is fundamentally the road map that bridges the gap between attaining spiritual salvation or damnation! In an effort for this concept to be realized, there are **"PERSONS OF AUTHORITYAND PERSONS IN AUTHORITY"** whose relationship, knowledge and expertise (in a religious doctrine) are accepted and considered exclusively abreast of "THE TRUTH" within this doctrine.

Consequently, many people (inclusive of our women) adore, attach and subjugate themselves to these individuals and their belief doctrines; that they lose sight of the subtle spiritual and psychological sexual dominance that trickle into the spiritual arena.

These **"PERSONS OF AUTHORITY AND PERSONS IN AUTHORITY"** do manifest many attributes that are considered welcoming, inspirational, appealing and spiritually empowering (by the religious members) that they intentionally capitalize and manipulate their followers in order to accomplish an "ungodly agenda."

In the case of our young men and women, many of them, who have had the opportunity of being "alter-boys, groomed to be deacons, ushers, church greeters or even members" have disclosed very gruesome, horrific, unwanted and forced sexual encounters with these "PERSONS OF AUTHORITY OR PERSONS IN AUTHORITY!"

These encounters have not only traumatized them for years but, have led to many of these youths becoming homosexuals, lesbians, trans-genders, introverted, not having healthy heterosexual relationship, depressed, frustrated, developing suicidal tendencies or even death.

The above manifestations are only the tip of the ice-berg, as it relates to "THE MASK BEFORE US!" In reference to the concept, "DOWN THERE or BACK THERE" as noted by numerous parents when it comes to our "PRIVATE PARTS," many children haven't been courageous or considered credible in disclosing such information.

Couple with the above statements, because many of these **"RELIGIOUS AUTHORITARIANS"** are highly respected and adored throughout circles and societies that the defamation of their characters become "unquestionable and unbelievable."

However, many of these "authoritarians" continue to perpetuate these abuses because they haven't been brought to justice for such sexual allegations. On the contrary, those who have have not been sanctioned properly because they are either transferred to a different religious jurisdiction, demoted to another order or financial settlements were made out of courts.

Evidently, the root of the problem still exists, within the fabric of the many religious sectors of our societies!

The magnitude and gravity of the preceding forces usually propel many of our women and men into an abyss of self-destruction! Too many times, in search of rehabilitation, the programs or strategies employed are not effective nor efficient in identifying the roots to these dis-eases!

Consequently, the vicious cycle of self-destruction becomes the manifestation of a deeper, rooted and seated social dysfunction!

Yes, as best intention these measures may be, the fueling factor in realizing this-is the money acquired from it! We must be cognizant of the fact that the health or well-being of these dis-eased individuals is not paramount to the local, state or federal entity! No! No! No!

It is a means to an end-economically, to satisfy and enlarge the interest of the socio-economic and geopolitical infrastructures that are in place and institutionalized!

The numerous health institutions and medications provided to our women and men, to combat these "psychological disorders" are given within the knowledge of not only their health risks but, the addictiveness to them!

Also, the provision of the social workers or professional personnel is not substantial enough to sensitize and administer genuine assistance to these individuals.

Granted, these "perpetuators or contributors" to the creation and transformation of one's "MASK" are equally-themselves, at a disadvantage!

The news media: internet, television, radio, racially and sexually driven songs or political infrastructures have been classified as the culprits to the solidification of the "THE MASK!" However, on the contrary, I beg to differ!

The overwhelming progression and denial of this heart-wrenching phenomenon are appalling!! Too many of our socio-economic and geopolitical high-powered leaders (both males and females) do take advantage of this phenomenon via deceits, bribes and other distasteful and evil acts.

In of themselves, the perpetuation and funneling of these heinous actions are greatly embedded from the lowest to the highest levels of and within every fabric of our social existence!

One may ask, "Aren't the powers that be, able to alleviate this madness? The answer is a resounding "Yes!" Then, the question begs, "Why not?" Simply put, they are benefitting from such acts of immorality! The detachment of and from our Creator and emotional senses themselves lead into the manifestations and amplification of our "HUMAN-ANIMAL WITHIN US!"

Too many times, the abusers become so stifled and suffocated in the relationships that their only thought of resolution is that of killing the person! On a personal level, that may seem very extreme! However, it is not any consolation to a person that is living in this life to say, "I understand your situation (when you haven't walked in that person's shoe,) or say, "God is going to punish him for you (when you are the one confronting this situation daily.)

RECOMMENDATIONS IN "BREAKING-FREE"

These individuals require urgent help and practical strategies that will afford them the ability to bring this to a reality! The following resolutions or recommendations are hereby submitted for such considerations

On the contrary, to either **SURVIVE DOMESTIC VIOLENCE OR BREAK THE CYCLE OF ABUSE,** I strongly recommend and submit the following practices for your kind consideration, self-internalization, and implementation in your relationships:

(1) Create a spiritual relationship with The Lord.
(2) Self-removal from person, place or situation.
(3) Become a member of a "SUPPORT GROUP or ORGANIZATION" that fosters restoration and self-healing from such.
(4) Take ownership for and of your deliverance and happiness.

The above factors may not resonate with everyone and don't have to be implemented in the order. However, those of you who desperately need to rid yourselves of such life, these measures are applicable, workable and proven very beneficial in achieving such a goal!

In deliberating on each point, here are the rationales in self-incorporating and implementing them in your lives:

1. **<u>CREATE A SPIRITUAL RELATIONSHIP WITH GOD</u>**

It must be noted that everyone has some level of spiritual belief, certain values or principles that are fundamentally embedded in their lives. These factors are the forces that provide them anchor, sense of direction and ultimately impact their interpretation and actions to life's circumstances.

If we look at the outrageous or heinous acts bestowed upon our women or men, in respect to **DOMESTIC VIOLENCE-** many people would say "suffering is the catalyst for spiritual growth or that's divine punishment for previous sins committed and consequently we are not loved by God!"

However, as Romans 8:38 (NIV) says "For neither death nor life, neither angels nor demons, neither the present nor the future, nor any powers, neither height nor depth, nor anything else in all creation, will not be able to separate us from the love of God that is in Christ Jesus or Lord!"

Violence is known to be a composite of biological, psychological and sociological factors basically that lead to shame, self-humiliation and destruction among others.

However, as a people, **DOMESTIC VIOLENCE or ABUSE** can be prevented by doing the reverse or just the opposite. The reverse or opposite include but not limited to: providing the individuals an atmosphere of "safety, love and connectivity."

These three concepts not only embody but also, heighten their self-worth, emotional attachment, empathy and avoidance to violence. Also, their responses to violence become less harsh in punishments because they are acting more because of love rather than emotions!" This technique then amplifies the incorporation of "calmness" and its introduction and application into the "breaking- free of the violence!"

In their assessment of Religious or Spiritual values in relationship to DOMESTIC VIOLENCE, one must be cognizant of the fact that they are the "CENTRAL or CORE" factors to the victims' understanding and behavioral responses to such.

The victims' inability to understand their biblical viewpoints, of whatever denomination could either impede or foster the "healing or breaking-free" of such a phenomenon.

The following scriptural quotations present a contradictory front or approach in many women's and men's endeavors to "**break-free**" of and from **DOMESTIC VIOLENCE**:

1. **(1 Cor. 7: 10) We must not separate ourselves from our husbands, but are bound for life by marriage.**
2. **(Ephesians 5:22-24) We should submit to our husbands as unto Christ.**
3. **(Matthew 18: 21-22) We should forgive each other and should repay evil with good.**

The above three quotations do present major limitations for anyone trying to "break-free," of or from the "DOMESTIC ABUSIVE RELATIONSHIP."

Why is that? The spiritual implications embedded here include: a sinful act would be committed and we may be punished by The Creator for separating or not forgiving each other.

These inherent psychological and spiritual factors greatly impose a sense of "fear" of losing God's BLESSINGS AND GRACE on one's life; in creating an automatic "sinful act."

Consequently, many partners in their relationships continue to be abused by the internalization of these philosophies of thoughts and actions in their lives.

On the contrary, THE LOVE OF SELF and SURVIVAL thereof, necessitate that embracing such thoughts are ludicrous! Why must one allow another to deprive him/her by granting such power to the abuser or at the expense of his/her happiness?

Evidently, the absence of "love-of-self" becomes over shadowed by the "love for the other party, fearful of spiritual repercussions or that of physical threats."

The SPIRITUAL RELATIONSHIP then, must be the bridge that gaps the thought to the reality of "breaking-free," via prayers! Many people have found out that there "exists a **Higher Force**" and their "**belief in a Higher FORCE**" governs our lives and contributes to our divine destiny!

Irrespective of the negative or positive forces that come from this **"HIGHER FORCE"** we all yield to that for "divine intervention."

The submission of "prayers" to our **"DIVINE CREATOR"** does yield great benefits in the transformation and removal of self from the situation (person, place or thing.)

The initiative and honest desire must be paramount in propelling this move to a reality. Granted, "The Lord or God", is not like "**IN-N-Out Burger" where you submit your orders and minutes later your requests are realized!**

> **NO, NO, NO!** Your prayers have to be continuous, have to be fervent and you have to submit and surrender yourself and issues to HIM/HER! Evidently, your personal initiatives have not provided any success in this process; so ultimately, DIVINE INTERVENTION is needed!

> In acknowledging that "This Force" is capable of realizing our desires, our "letting-go" must be first and foremost accepted and placed or "handed-over" to "That Force;" to work it out or resolve the concern.

> Many times, frustrations, depressions, tear drops and sleepless nights will become part of the set-backs or even create disbelief; in the length of time your request seems to be unanswered.

However, do not be dismayed, "The FORCE/ FORCES THAT BE" are working on your behalf behind the scenes!

In keeping with the trend of thoughts, there is not any "specific or time line that will usher in the desired answer /answers. Again, this delay or waiting phase may further aggravate the impatience factor! However, the need for this "divine intervention" provides the victim or abused party patience and trust upon the "Higher Force."

It must be noted, the answer/s do surface or present themselves so sudden and unexpectedly! This could be in the form of a dream, a message, a person, location or situation like a "light bulb" inspiration! These revelations do evidently provide "extra-ordinary strength, courage, insight, invigoration, inspiration and sense of direction" in embarking on the realization of such an endeavor.

It is imperative to note, that many battered and abused heterosexuals, run to the religious organizations or denominations; as a "safety-net" from DOMESTIC VIOLENCE!

Their trust and belief in this "Spiritual Environment" does provide them the courage and strength in confiding in the religious leaders. Many of them have **found and gotten the support, guidance and words of inspiration from these institutions; in "breaking-free" from the abuses. They have attributed this "breaking-free" to (1) Fervent Prayers, (2) Personal choice and decision to abandon relationship/s, (3) Support group and (4) Provision of a specific date or time to "break-free!"**

The above factors, irrespective of the order employed do hinge on three scriptural quotations incorporated by the prospective abusers or victims:

(1) (Hebrews 11:1) NIV "Now Faith is the substance of things hoped for, the evidence of things not seen."

(2) (Proverbs 3: 5 & 6) NIV "Trust in the Lord with all your heart and lean not unto your own understanding, in all your ways submit to Him, and He will make your path straight.

(3) (Hebrews 11: 6-8) KJV. "And without Faith it is impossible to please God, because anyone who comes to Him must believe that He exists and that He rewards those who earnestly seek him.

The premise and common thread that ties these victims or abusers to the quotations is **"FAITH!"** Many of them have relied and put their total **"deliverance"** on the assurance that their efforts are and will not be in vain! Why? Because they "trust, trust or have faith" in the Almighty God-who is the Author and Finisher of their Faith! They take Him at His words; for His words do not return void!

However, some victims or abusers of DOMESTIC VIOLENCE that have approached some "Faith Communities" for safety or as a place of sanctuary" have not been so successful. On the contrary, these communities have subjected them to thoughts of: it's their duty as wives/ husbands to stay in the marriage, worker more or harder at making the marriage work, or even pray for guidance, strength to subdue or overcome the abuse or abuser.

Too often, the above factors lead to more of the "Domestic Violence" or even physical death! This does sound quite far-fetch but, the defense mechanism of one, after so much abuse does lend itself to responses that are sudden, detrimental and deadly. The repercussions, then, are translated into these actions that ultimately can't be taken back!

Evidently, then, the choice between employing the first four factors as oppose to the latter does become a matter of the abuser's religious beliefs, desire to incorporate and employ them or not!

2. **SELF-REMOVAL FROM PERSON, PLACE OR SITUATION**
The above concept of "**Self-removal from the person, place or situation**" is easier said than done! Why is that? A couple factors such

as: fear, emotional ties, children and mutual debts do present major limitations in executing this act.

Let us examine two of the above forces more in depth.

(1) **FEAR-** The element of **"fear"** usually impedes one party from "breaking-free" or withdrawing one-self from the forces of Domestic Violence! The abused is usually "fearful" of the repercussions that could be imposed upon him or her in the process. That could include: stalking, threating to kill either party, taking children away, and not providing for home (economically,) infidelity or uncertainty of the future.

These forces greatly undermine the person in the decision process and execution thereof. In understanding the magnitude and gravity of your life being taken away, by your abuser, does more than often binds one to seriously rethink such a move. For many victims of Domestic Violence, be it males or females, the losing of one's life is not worth leaving the bond.

Consequently, they continue to live within this entrapment called a "World of Misery, Frustration, Confusion and Emptiness!"

Irrespective of the duration of the relationship (either via death, relocation or abandonment) the abused usually tend to console himself or herself with "it's better to be alive than dead!"

The lacking of the courage, strength and determination not found within, greatly restrict and impede the realization of such desire.

(2) **Children**-It has been noted that many parents have and are sacrificing their emotional, physical, economic, spiritual and material happiness for the over-all well-being of their children! Whatever that may mean to you, Domestic Violence is inclusive therein.

The realization of the parents not wanting to see their children crying, sad, transforming in "monsters" at home or schools, don't want them to be raised by another man or woman, or children accusing them of destroying their future (because of break-up or separation, or parents committing suicide or homicide;) many parents resort to humbling themselves by staying and enduring the abuses so as not to see or put their children in such state. Also, not to personally experience the hurts and pains that the above forces overwhelming would cause; if such an act would be executed.

Unfortunately, this trend of thought and action usually tend to be counter- productive! This is so because by either parent staying, in the relationship, the abuse does not deescalate but, increases due to unsolved anger, scars, wounds and pains that are still embedded within the victims mind or body.

Also, the presence of unresolved issues and tension within the couple or children find themselves resurfacing and undermining the rekindling process. The children, then, find themselves becoming either pawns or contributors to further problems in the homes.

PLACE- In relation to **"place,"** many times this movement does become a bit easier to execute than moving away from the person! The ability to relocate often times presents the abused better options of places or sanctuary!

This move could be another state, city or county. It doesn't mean that the abused can't be tracked down but, the frequency of interconnection is greatly limited. Also, the abused can change name in an effort to greatly reduce the possibility of being contacted or tracked down.

The transition of location also can provide the abused an opportunity of restarting and restructuring his or her life. In such process, the baggages of the past can be left behind and a new identity taken on in proceeding with one's life.

Too often, when this transition occurs the victim finds it refreshing, invigorating and self-full filling! The ability to regroup, create new friends, find a new job and even become part of a support group do present an alleviation to the continuous torture or exposure to such abuse.

In light of this, the **"break-free"** process does provide for a firmer ground via this act to connect with other law enforcement agencies and institutions; in an effort to provide a sense of security. Also, the possibility of meeting or interacting with this person is further limited; especially if no knowledge of address, name, or place of contact.

Many abused victims utilize this strategy, quicker, than that of just detaching him or herself from the abuser. In an effort to escape such harsh realities, of DOMESTIC ABUSE, the next step is that of removing one's self from the SITUATION!

SITUATION- The **situation** does provide the medium which embodies the elements of **DOMESTIC ABUSE**. However, in removing one-self from the person and place; usually allows better avoidance of the situation.
Sometimes, if the abused is not careful, he or she may resort to employing those very abusive tactics on those who are subservient to him or her. This move is usually deployed as a "reversed attack" on the less fortunate.

However, if the abused party is genuinely relinquishing him or herself of the negative forces rendered due to DOMESTIC ABUSE, then this move becomes helpful in the **"healing"** process.

To further solidify this act, the removal from the situation can greatly be **reinforced by becoming a part of "SUPPORTIVE GROUP" and not entertaining relationships that feed upon or foster those negative behavioral patterns.**

DIVORCE

The inclusion of Divorce, as a "break-free" tool or resolution to an abusive or Domestic Violent Relationship is an alternative strategy; that is legally binding in detaching the parties from each other physically. Also, embedded within the judgment are orders or mandates that restrict parties from interacting or disturbing each other.

However, there may exists major issues of misunderstanding (after the divorce decree is made) if children, finances, or assets are involved- during the tenure of the marriage.

The incorporation of one or more of the Alternative Dispute Resolution strategies: Negotiation, Mediation, Litigation or Arbitration or combination of all) are fundamentally the fabric that make up the divorce proceedings; leading ultimately to the divorce decree or judgment.

Depending on the **magnitude and gravity** of the major disputes or issues- that determine the strategy or strategies employ. A brief definition on each strategy as provided by Wikipedia is as follow:

Mediation:
It is the attempt by a third party or person (that is non-party to the case) to help disputing parties in a disagreement to hear one another, to minimize the harm that can come from the disagreement (e.g. hostility or "demonizing" of the parties) to maximize any area of agreement and to find a way of preventing the areas of misunderstanding from interfering with the process of seeking a compromise or mutually agreed outcome.

Negotiation:
Is a dialogue between two or more people/parties intended to reach a mutually beneficial resolution to a problem. This beneficial

outcome can be for all parties involved, or just one or some of them, in situation in which a good outcome for one/some, excludes the possibility of a desired result for the other/others.

Arbitration

It is the submission of a dispute to an unbiased third person designated by the parties to the controversy/disagreement, who agree in a divorce to comply with the award-a decision to be issued after a hearing at which both parties have an opportunity to be heard on the issues disputed upon.

Litigation

This is a legal method for settling controversial or disputes between and among parties, organizations and the state. In litigation, a case (called suit or lawsuit) is brought before a court of law suitably empowered (having the jurisdiction) to hear the case, by the parties involved (the litigants for resolution (the judgment.)

The divorce judgment or decree could be granted based on "Domestic Violence!" Sometimes, the term Domestic Violence is alternately called "Cruel Treatment," which is a composite of both mental and physical abuse.

The dissolution for many relationships, usually birth from matters or issues that weren't openly and honestly taken seriously or dealt with, by one or both parties. Too often, the inability (for either party) to confront or address them does contribute to the escalation and ultimately the "break-up" of the bond.

Irrespective of the disclosures of one's desires, dislikes, pains, frustrations, aspirations or passions to the other party -the insensitivity, non-willingness to work or change actions or course of actions and inconsideration (of either one) do usually undermine the betterment or progress of the relationship.

The disadvantage of not being supportive (in one or all the needs to the relationship) compounded by the domestic violence can lend itself to one gravitating towards the "break-free" process, much faster. Also, if there exist lies, deceits, infidelity and manipulation of whatever kind, these too can ignite a friction of unprecedented catastrophic proportion in the relationship.

It is evident that because many couples within their relationship do not take a more proactive role and a broader view of themselves and their responsibilities in the marriages; they (relationship) gradually spiral into an abyss of emptiness, loneliness and insignificance! Once this trend continues and becomes the "norm" of and within the relationship, it ultimately climaxes into "divorce" or "break-up" of the bond.

3. JOIN A SUPPORTIVE GROUP OR ORGANIZATION

The importance of a Supportive Group has always been misunderstood! Many abused individuals, irrespective of gender or gender-orientation, have seen this body or institution as non-productive and incapable of solving or satisfying their needs.

It must be noted however, that SUPPORT GROUPS OR ORGANIZATIONS ARE NOT LIMITED TO STRUCTURES BUT TO INDIVIDUALS! These knowledgeable and qualified individuals are not only there to share their personal experiences but, also to provide positive alternatives in the resolution of these domestic Many victims have proclaimed and flocked into institutions that haven't afforded them substantial help; as relates to self-empowerment or self-transformation for their betterment in relationship to DOMESTIC VIOLENCE! Those may be issues that contribute to the destruction of the relationships.

Coupled with the above statement, the incorporation of the law enforcement agencies (such as the police) does bring awareness and recorded information to the existence of the abuse.

Too often, the non-disclosure of this information to the proper authorities or fear of the police does contribute to the escalation of the DOMESTIC VIOLENCE! On the contrary, if such atrocities are brought to the attention of these entities, then legal and professional interventions can be had!

It is imperative to note, "**SILENCE**" means consent! The "consent" may not be welcomed but enforced and applied by the perpetuator as long as no "intervention" is made.

SUPPORTIVE GROUPS OR ORGANIZATIONS THAT CAN AID IN THE HEALING PROCESS INCLUDE BUT, NOT LIMITED TO: CHURCHES, WOMEN AGAINST VIOLENCE, FAMILY AND LEGAL AID, HUMAN RIGHTS ORGANIZATIONS AND THE LIKE.

The important thing is to "**GET HELP**" in confronting the fears, hurts and pains ushered in by the DOMESTIC ABUSE! Yes, the disclosure of these very sensitive and heart wrenching experiences does make one "vulnerable!"

Vulnerability opens the doors for criticisms, ostracization, degradation and even humiliation! However, the acquisition of a better life-style and peace of mind are among the benefits of embracing and submitting to these realities! If the pains and hurts are stifled and suffocated in the abused without an outlet, the person becomes like a pressure cooker and ultimately can explode into a more destructive individual on a personal or societal aspect.

In an effort to curb such a harsh reality, the need for intervention of the SUPPORT GROUPS OR ORGANIZATIONS IS IMPERATIVE! Often times, the abused in a DOMESTIC VIOLENT relationship believes that he or she is mentally, physically and emotionally strong to overcome these hurdles or negative forces! That may be so but, not many can survive the tide.

Some may even believe that money can alleviate the stress, hurts, and pains or eliminate the person; that is causing the violence. However, that is only a temporary fix. The SUPPORT GROUPS OR ORGANIZATIONS then, can empower, enhance and structurally direct the abused or abuser in positive alternative strategies in curbing the DOMESTIC VIOLENCE!

4. Take Responsibility For Personal Happiness

Throughout the birth, development and maturity of any relationship, there exists a fundamental connectivity to all three called "attachment." This "attachment" possesses "tentacles" that feed upon the very fabric our emotional, psychological, social, spiritual, physical, economic and political foundations of our existence.

These "tentacles" once embedded into our socio-economic and geo-political structures not only define us but, we become subjugated and obligated to them!

The obligation and subjugation are not based on immaturity, intelligence, stupidity or inability to sustain one-self! No, No, No! Those two forces become the "norm" because either party (in the relationship) becomes co-dependent on each other.

The Webster's Universal College Dictionary defines "Co-dependent" as follows "of or pertaining to a relationship in which one person is physically or psychologically addicted, as to alcohol or gambling and the other person is psychologically dependent on the first in an unhealthy way."

In many domestic relationships, the forces of "Co-dependency" become the birth and breeding ground of and for DOMESTIC VIOLENCE or DOMESTIC ABUSE! Too often, either party doesn't "TAKE RESPONSIBILITY FOR PERSONAL HAPPINESS! The infringement, intrusion, and destruction of and into one's life is then manifested into that of the "Name-Blame-Game!"

Ironically, neither party does take ownership or responsibility for or to the demise or break-up of the relationship but, is seen as the victim of it or person. The foregoing philosophy of thought is further amplified in the abuse or abuser's life-style becoming more verbally or physically escalated to that of the "usual or norm" in resolving issues of misunderstanding.

Irrespective of the situation or circumstance, the source of one's happiness should ultimately be determined by the abused, instead of the abuser! As the late, great **Bod Nesta Marley** said, "**None but ourselves can free our minds; Love the life you live. Live the life you Love; Open your eyes, look within. Are you satisfied with the life you living; Get up stand up. Stand up for your rights. Get up, stand up. Don't give up the fight!**"

The above quotations are the foundations to the self-actualization process that Maslow spoke about in his Hierarchy of Needs. Also, it is the embodiment of one's decision to take personal accountability and responsibility of his/her happiness.

This self-liberation can only be materialized if the zeal is internalized and seen **as worthy for the fight; no matter at what cost or sacrifice may be required! The transference of one's personal power to another, as relates to your happiness, undermines the self-realization to such a vision.**

Lord Acton, the historian and moralist, expressed to Bishop Mandell Creighton in 1887, "Power tends to corrupt, and absolute power corrupts absolutely. Great men are almost always bad men." Also, the above thought was the central theme in the book, Animal Farm by George Orwell. Consequently, the provision of one to determine or have total jurisdiction for and over one's happiness is opening the doors to abuse.

In our society but, more specifically in DOMESTIC RELATIONSHIPS, the decision making or control within many of the homes is unilaterally made. Too often, the male dominance is greater; which leads to bullying, physical, emotional, economic or psychological abuse.

The emergence of a defense mechanism by the female counterpart or less confrontational or pacific partner, usually translates into verbal or physical altercation and abuse.

In an effort for one to be assertive and proactive to this ability, of taking ownership for "personal happiness" he or she must be cognizant that the future hinges on the choices of the past and present.

The concepts of "I should, I could or I would" are statements embedded in thoughts or actions that ultimately manifest themselves either positively or negatively-if not taken.

It must be noted, however, that because DOMESTIC VIOLENCE many times lead to death, there is no taking back of such thoughts or actions. No words of sympathy, empathy can bring back a life once the blow is struck.

CONCLUSION

The overwhelming manifestations of Domestic Abuse/Violence have birth this book into life. Too many individuals, irrespective of color, gender, creed or race, suppress and disguise the negative impacts inflicted upon them in many subtle and harmful ways. Consequently, these internal pains, hurts and self-degradation become transformative forces in the person's new identity that solidifies itself into a "quiet storm." I, too, have been on the receiving end of the impacts of this harsh reality that have contributed to "**The Disfigured Mask**."

The denial to the "truth" trickles within every fabric of our human existence; with the home being its birth place and breeding ground! Too often, the abuse/abuser of DOMESTIC VIOLENCE live a "lie and life" of co-dependency in spite of the abuse.

The tool/weapon of choice in "resolving" the domestic issues or problems is "SEX!" However, in knowing that that is a temporary fix- only lends itself to a deeper and more severe rupturing of the relationship.

It is a given, "SEX or LOVE-MAKING" is critical to the relationship but, it doesn't resolve major issues that are swept under the rug or un-dealt with.

The perpetuation and heightened intensity of these "learnt and negative behaviors" do often translate into more physical and emotional scars, that aren't vivid to the naked eyes.

If positive and effective measures or course of action are not taken, to curb this harsh reality, then the vicious cycle of DOMESTIC VIOLENCE/ABUSE continues. Consequently, these individuals' behavioral patterns become so transformed and disguised that" THE DISFIGURED MASK" is birth into being.

ACKNOWLEDGEMENT

TO GOD BE THE HONOR, GLORY AND PRAISE IN THE ACCOMPLISHMENT OF YET ANOTHER MILESTONE IN AND OF MY LIFE!

The wealth of inspiration and knowledge provided and experienced from the "storms of life" were the foundation and pillar to the birth of this book.

I am greatly indebted to MY NUBIAN QUEEN, MELVA BUCHANAN-HARRIS, without whose valuable support and continuous encouragement this book would not have been realized.

Also, special "Thank you" goes out to my publication company, XLIBRIS! The staff has been very professional and resourceful in every way in the publication-of now my fourth book, "THE DISFIGURED MASK!"